THE GOOD PARENT AND THE HAPPY CHILD

"Nicole's evident passion for children and parents' development shines through into script with this great body of work. This book is candid, straightforward and satisfyingly honest about the highs, lows and the joys of parenting.

As there is no definitive way on how to raise your kids, this book will give you an almost perfect guide both Mothers and Fathers can refer to over and over again"

- Terence Wallen, Best Selling Author, Humanitarian, Entrepreneur

THE GOOD PARENT AND THE HAPPY CHILD

A Guide for Parents, Caregivers

and Early Years Consultants

NICOLE BENNETT BLAKE

THE GOOD PARENT AND *THE HAPPY CHILD*

© Copyright (2022 by DMJ Publishing) by (Nicole Bennett Blake)
All rights reserved.

ISBN: 978-1-7399029-3-3

All rights reserved. No part of this publication may be reproduced, distributed, or transmitted in any form or by any means, including photocopying, recording, or other electronic or mechanical methods, without the prior written permission of the publisher, except in the case of brief quotations embodied in critical reviews and certain other noncommercial uses permitted by copyright law.

Published in Birmingham, England by DMJ Publishing.
www.dmjpublishing.co.uk

DEDICATION

I dedicate this book to all parents, caregivers, grandparents and Early Year Consultants everywhere. I commiserate you who are parents or form part of the parenting team for children. Whether you are part of a two-unit parent (Nuclear) family or are a lone parent depending on family community or working in the children sector. All of you who are raising children, this life journey is no walk in the park. Most would argue that it is the most challenging yet rewarding job.

Without a doubt, it is the most important!

Foreword

To parents everywhere, a child's first and most important teacher is one that influence, and lead by example! This is the motto Nicole takes in supporting parents develop the strategies to ensure their children achieve their potential.

It has been a pleasure to know Nicole Bennett Blake since 2021 and working as her agent has been an absolute epic journey. I believe in supporting authors to use a book as a marketing tool and income accelerator. I have spoken to over three million people and teach them how to align, brand and attract prospective clients to their business using their book as a lead magnet.

Nicole is one of those who took up the challenge to use me as her agent to accomplish such a challenge. She has dedicated herself to be innovative, professional and consistent in pursuing her ambition for parents to build a solid parent and child relationship. In her book, she has highlighted key factors: foundation of communication between parents and child. She focuses on learning how to listen, allowing the child to express their feeling and addressing those feelings. She also talks about parents being open to understand their value and also to understand that they are loved.

The book demonstrates how to accept that deeper relationship to enjoy being who they are which teaches the child the fundamentals of establishing 'the foundation' of communication to be built upon. Not all parents can do this under the same roof; however, with support or professional intervention, relationships can and do improve.

The Parent and The Happy Child author, Nicole Bennett-Blake, stresses that children learn within the boundaries of a healthy parent and child relationship. A child's ability to love, accept love, validate their emotions, and comply to boundaries, are all part of their holistic development. The greater the parent-child relationship, the better the child will be at following rules, self-regulating and communicating.

Problem solving is the principal thread through Nicole's book. The key to The Parent and The Happy Child is to master the tips offered consistently being opened to discuss with your child any issues raised; this will, no doubt, continue to nurture your relationship much deeper and leave a legacy to be passed on. Children enjoy being who they are, so support and help them develop. Setting boundaries, along with having rules and consequences are the key factors mentioned in her book.

Nicole is an expert in the field of childcare, she has been a social worker for over fifteen years and a nursery manager for over a decade. She has used her experience and knowledge gain to support parents, children and other professionals working with children in ensuring that there are clear lines of communication and consistency and that children are treated with respect. Her passion is mainly to see children strive, support the next generation to grow up knowing how to love, show empathy, show their emotions and not being introverts. She would like to see the next generation of parents who can respond appropriately and affectionately. Nicole is of the opinion that this present generation is the one who needs to break the mold and be a bridge between the older generation and the next generation and to shape their future.

GERRY ROBERTS

Black Cards Books

Table of Contents

Introduction	11
Chapter One: Being Pregnant	14
Chapter Two: First-time Mum	22
Chapter Three: Understanding How Your Child Develops	34
Chapter Four: Being an Effective Parent	43
Chapter Five: Values are For Life	49
Chapter Six: Critical And Engaging Child	57
Chapter Seven: How Much Is Healthy	68
Chapter Eight: The Pizzazz Child	85
Chapter Nine: Technology and The Digital World	97
Chapter Ten: Shaping Future Parent	105
Conclusion	111
Bibliography	112
Acknowledgements	114
Resources the Author Recommends	116
Testimonials	118
About The Author	120

INTRODUCTION

Every parent I know believes it is important to be a good parent and wants their child to be happy. The surprising truth is, irrespective of age, becoming a mother is a daunting experience, so getting it right takes practice, consistency, and responsibility.

Most of the time, parents succeed at this but not always. Sometimes we unwittingly demonstrate the very behaviour we want our children to avoid, or the mistakes we perceived that our parents made while rearing us.

In spite of these challenges, most young women dream of the day when they become mothers and how they would do things different from the way they were brought up. They pledge that they would not make the same mistakes their parents made, during their own childhood.

Parenting is never a bed of roses; for some parents, it is an uphill battle.

My book is to support young mothers, older mothers or parents who need support to grow their child in an enabling environment. It will enable them to meet the needs of their children while at the same time enjoy motherhood; it will allow them to step away from the pressure of daily life, so to speak, and enjoy being a parent.

This book will equip, educate, and support parents, caregivers and early years practitioners who are bringing up or working with children that are experiencing challenges. This includes children who are fussy eaters, clingy or just finding it difficult to settle. It explores ways to connect or reconnect with your child and highlights effective ways to help children explore their strengths and begin their journey on the way to approaching life with confidence.

The advice given in this book is what I have shared on numerous occasions with parents of children I worked with and they all found the advice useful. Not every suggestion works for all but rest assured that trial and error will prove which option will work for you.

My mother gave birth to me at forty years of age. I was the youngest of thirteen children born to my parents. Growing up in such a large family and having young cousins, nephews and aunts was a bonus. I spent my childhood and first half of my adulthood in Jamaica before immigrating.

I immigrated to the United Kingdom at the age of twenty-four and gained my first employment in a children's home working with the Salvation Army. Getting married and raising three children of my own has been a gift that supported my parenting skills; it has given me a love for children and paved the pathway of my career thus far.

It led to me attending university to become trained as a Social Worker and after completing university, I worked for a number of years for the local authority as a Social Worker for children. During this period, I completed numerous trainings, for example, Child Development, Safeguarding, Speech and Language, amongst other relevant training. I have since completed a second degree in Early Childhood Status Practitioner.

This has led me to successfully owning and managing a children's nursery for over fifteen years. During those years, I have supported a vast number of parents with their children's learning and behaviour. This included parents whose children are fussy eaters, parents with children who need to develop their independent skills, high energy children and children who have speech delay. It was always paramount that I supported both parent and child to triumphantly reach the aim of verbal communication, by encouraging development of their children's speech and for each child to grow in all areas through their P.S.E.D (personal, social, educational and development).

All parents want their children to flourish with good health, to be safe and happy. To do well academically and make the most of leisure opportunities, hobbies, and interest.

We want our children to be equipped to lead independent lives and to make their way as adults in higher education, obtain good careers and jobs, and be financially secure. Also, if they themselves become parents, we will ensure they receive early, sensitive, and effective support. Sometimes, as parents, we get it wrong by doing the very thing we warn our children not to do. Often, we overcompensate the nature over nurturing of the child. This is an issue I want to explore: which is the concept to see how we can develop a balance of both, and the place each play in child development.

One example of bad behaviour that most of us as parents are guilty of is when, from time to time, we scream at a four-year-old to stop yelling in the middle of the supermarket. Those mistakes are made in a moment of frustration, and good parents will realise right away what they have done wrong.

We want them to have good quality care that will support them as they make their way through childhood into adulthood and beyond. This is why, globally, we recognise the importance of supporting the development of a positive identity in the diverse communities in which we live and grow.

The information in my book will give insight and strategies based upon proven practical strategies drawn from years of working with children. Helping to build communication skills, their personal, emotional, and self-care skills, these allow children to grow up with confidence, while parents discover the strategies to bond with their child. Start breaking unhealthy habits, establish safe boundaries, and connect or reconnect with your child so you can enjoy spending time with them, while finding time for yourself. Do not extend the problem: the earlier you have the information to support your child through their early years' foundation stage of life, the more equipped you will be to guide them through teenage years and adulthood.

Are you ready to boost your parenting skills and create an enabling home environment, and a lasting bond with your child?

May I encourage you do not wait too long because, as the first educator of your child, there is no better time to start than now.

The sooner you get a copy of my book, "The Good Parents and The *Happy Child*," the happier you will be in becoming a good parent with happy children.

If you have a baby, young children, or work with children, then my book is for you. My book is a clear guide for parents, caregivers, and early year consultants.

CHAPTER ONE: BEING PREGNANT

"Parenting" is naturally thought of as being a wonderful thing. Being pregnant is most women's dream, especially if they are in a loving, stable relationship. They want nothing more than to express their love for their partner by having a child.

They dream of the day when they become a mother; this should be a natural aspect of life and its continuation but, for some, it does not come naturally or the road to parenting comes through a variety of paths.

Depending on your chosen path, it can be a walk in the park while for others conceiving can be an emotional challenge. So, at what age should women start to give attention to this part of their lives?

Some women get to a certain stage in life and decide it is time to have a child, and that's okay. But depending on the age of the woman, this can have many setbacks and health risk.

Is it better to have children when we are young or when we are older and financially secure?

Or when we have climbed the ladder of success and have everything in place to financially provide for a child?

The fact that some women make this decision, and it doesn't work in their favour, does not mean this will be the case for every woman that does. So where do we draw the balance? How can we be one hundred percent sure that our pregnancy will be a success and, at the end, we will have a beautiful healthy child and the support to raise the child?

Even a healthy young lady can suffer difficulties as not every pregnancy will live up to the expectation.

Dreams do not always come true; some women have difficult pregnancies, while others are unable to conceive and others suffer miscarriages, but then go on to have children. I respect medical guidelines about older women having children and the risk they face having child after they have reached age forty and beyond. The possibility of the child having health needs are greater in those cases than when a younger woman is having a child but we must admit this is not always the case.

There is always the possibility that a woman in her forties and over can carry and give birth to a healthy child. The benefits of making decisions about your body is still a woman's choice.

Some will argue that they would rather carry their baby than have it aborted because of medical advice given, with the possibility the child may have some form of disability or health issues due to the age of the mother.

Just as parenting has its ups and downs, so does pregnancy.

My first pregnancy went smoothly; I hardly had any pregnancy sickness. I completed my first trimester and second trimester before anyone knew I was pregnant. I gained no weight at all in my stomach, so I was able to enjoy my pregnancy, especially during the summer of 1991, which was the most incredible thing I ever experience. I was able to go for long walks, the nights were cool and resulted in me having peaceful sleep at nights. Getting on public transport, people would let me have their seat, hold doors for me and help to carry my shopping. This was a pleasant treat, which I enjoyed.

Going to my antenatal care for check-ups during my first pregnancy and being able to discuss with the nurse the different stages of changes my body was experiencing was, to some extent, the highlight of my pregnancy. One of the things I was most worried about during my pregnancy was that I was going to end up with stretch marks on my stomach. This was not the case, because I did not gain any excess weight during my entire pregnancy. When I was around my second trimester and approximately twenty-eight weeks pregnant, the doctors were concerned that I was not gaining sufficient weight and thought they would need to deliver the baby early. However, this did not happen, and I carried my baby to full-term; she was born at forty weeks, weighing seven pounds, ten ounces.

When I was told my baby's due date, I was excited and started to make preparation for my baby's arrival.

The good news is that with my second pregnancy, because of my knowledge of mindfulness and complementary therapies, I was able use my therapeutic self-help tools to manage my symptoms.

My second pregnancy was completely different from my first pregnancy, I was sick from the word go. I was unable to keep anything down, I just felt tired and had no energy whatsoever. It was not just the morning sickness—it was all day and night sickness—hence why it is now called pregnancy sickness. I never felt worse in my life: I was constantly hungry and everything I ate refused to settle. I was completely starving during my second pregnancy.

My friend, Michele (owner of micheleakester-marsh.com), who is a pregnancy coach, informed me during research for my book that during her first pregnancy, she suffered with Hyperemesis Gravidarum which is a severe form of nausea and vomiting during pregnancy. This can lead to dehydration, malnutrition, and weight loss. This condition is different from pregnancy sickness (commonly known as morning sickness). She reported that this condition causes many women to require hospitalisation during pregnancy. She suffered mildly compared to many other pregnant women but even so, in her words, "It was horrendous."

Every woman's pregnancy experience is different: some may experience fatigue and sickness, day or night, for some time. In fact, women have had experience of miscarriage so many times that they give up on the idea of ever conceiving or even being able to carry a baby to full-term.

There are also some women who make the decision not to conceive, but to adopt. Whichever route you may have taken that brought you into being a mother, let me take this time to congratulate you and encourage you for taking such a brave step.

Parenting is not always easy: it can be hard work, while at the same time it is amazingly rewarding to hold your child in your hand for the first time. It is fulfilling to watch your child grow and develop, to be able to support your child as they go through all the stages of development and gain all the skills to be independent.

Patterns of parenting style are diverse and there is no one perfect way to bring up children. It is never about "one style suits all": good parenting involves a combination of knowledge, skills, trial and error. Understanding at first how to hold a new-born baby to changing and settling the baby to sleep are all things a new mum has to learn, which at times can be challenging.

Growing up in Jamaica, in a family of thirteen children with both my parents, had its own challenges. Often, there was sibling rivalry, among other things. As children, we fail to live up to the expected standards set by our parents. Staying out late without parents' permission was unthinkable and when broken, it brought its own set of consequences.

My parents were at times challenged by us, so it was difficult to keep a tight hold on what we got up to. My father was an authoritarian parent and had high expectations of his children. He had set rules that were strictly not to be broken by any of us.

My father's mindset was that when we did things outside the family home (in public) that did not meet with his approval, we were bringing shame on the family name. So, we had to always bear in mind how we conducted ourselves when away from home.

So, since I grew up with both parents, you would think they should be able to manage. However, more often than not, they were at their wits end about what to do with us and the challenges that sometimes followed us home.

One of the challenges my parents faced was when we got to a certain age and thought it was okay to "back talk" to our parents. No parent likes when their child "talks back" to them. I grew up in a time when children were seen and not heard, so even the idea of us given our parents our ideas and thoughts on a topic or subject was not acceptable.

Another challenge was the constant jealousy and fighting between siblings, also us getting into fights with the neighbours' children. It was a constant headache for my parents having a barrage of parents coming to the family home with complaint about the damage we caused during fights.

My father had to pay for school bags, books and often school uniforms that got torn and damaged during fights.

Just imagine a single parent with no support and having to make the decisions that should be made by two people. Of course, parenting is an uphill battle but we all must keep working at it and hope we are doing the best for our child or children.

Asking for help should never be seen as a negative step or a failure, but rather as a step towards taking responsibility and understanding your child.

One of the drawbacks to parenting is that the minute we become parents, we forget that we existed as an individual before our children came along. We start to neglect who we are, and our child becomes our only focus. We seldom find or give any thought to "me time, or personal time."

Being available for yourself has its benefits. One of the benefits of having "me time" is that it gives you space to recharge your battery and to catch up with friends. Finding time for yourself allows you to do some of the things you enjoy doing. In today's world, taking time for yourself is looked upon as been selfish, when there is work to do such as taking care of the family, cooking meals, etc. The truth is that, without self-care, you're not giving yourself a fighting chance to be healthy and you will experience burnout. Spending time away from your child from an early age allows your child to start understanding that there will be times when you are not going to be with them, but you will return. The idea of attachment theory allows the child to develop a sense of security to their caregiver. Allowing your child to spend time with our people will help to develop secure attachment in the knowledge that when they are away from you will always come back. In the long run, this will have a positive impact on your child's psychosocial development and will far outweigh not spending time away from your child.

In my field of work, I have been working with children and parents for over twenty years. I am of the opinion that parents who, from an early age (infancy), leave their babies with a sitter or extended family members are supporting their children to become secure in their attachment. This allows the child to be more skilled forming relationship with their peers.

CHAPTER TWO: First-time Mum

Parenting is hard, especially for first-time mums; it is a matter of learning as you go along, and there are so many things you have to learn. No one has yet produced a manual on how to do so successfully. Feeling overwhelmed or depressed at times is completely normal as your body goes through a series of emotions, as does your newborn baby.

Having a new addition to the family for some parents means extra pressure—both emotionally and financially. Not everyone can cope with the increase in responsibility. We learn that as mothers, our basic, primal instinct as a parent is to protect your child.

How do you go about doing that?

You start at the point of your knowledge of what you know about childcare and your understanding of their needs. Having a baby does not always have a fairytale ending. Babies do not come with instructions, so no one really knows where to begin, until they are holding their child in their hands. Establishing sleep routine and eating habits, while at the same time dealing with keeping the rest of the family clean and the house tidy, along with all the other roles a mother does, motherhood can be a bit tricky. Not to mention the fact that our bodies' hormones do a see-saw from time to time, Our basic primal instinct as a parent is to protect your child

During my first experience of being a mum, coming home from the hospital with a newborn baby that was completely relying on me was daunting. I had so many unanswered questions. How do

I know if I am doing things the right way? What if I drop her? All these and more questions kept popping into my head. Conceiving my first child at age twenty-five, I was not prepared for childbirth, or raising a child. I was away from my parents and living in a foreign country with little support; I had no clue what to do. Closing my front door to the world and holding that child in my hands evoked a lot of emotions, for which I was not prepared.

However, I understood the importance of being a mum, from my mother's point of view. Watching my mother taking care of the family by ensuring that meals were prepared on time, the home was kept tidy and dirty laundry washed were just a few of the many tasks she did for us.

I was not prepared for the feeling of loneliness or self-doubt that overwhelmed me. So, I knew I had a choice to make, I had to do the best I could for myself and my daughter. But I did not feel like I could share my thoughts with anyone. I felt like people would think I was just being silly, so I kept my thoughts to myself.

On good days, I would think about people younger than myself, that I was acquainted with, who have children. I would reflect on their parenting and took courage in the fact that if they could do it, so could I.

Having my first child and learning to care for myself and a newborn baby was initially difficult. Living in London, away from my parents, was exceedingly difficult. Emotionally, I felt I could not cope on my own. Not having a more experienced mother to guide me on what to do and how to do things was my greatest worry.

I had to learn on the job, so most things I learnt by trial and error. For the first few weeks, I would sit by my child's bed and watch her sleep just to make sure she was still breathing. I would put a mirror under her nose to check her breathing: this was how worried I was. Gradually, as weeks turned into months, I became more confident in my new role as a mother and started to relax until I found I could do chores in the home without watching her constantly, when she was sleeping. Irrespective of how many dishes were in the sink or whether the laundry was waiting to be done, at first, I found it hard to leave her by herself. If you see that you are not managing, ask for help; ask other family members or friends as it is a matter of protecting your health and mental health.

Selfcare Is Not Selfish

Your role as a parent is first to understand who you are and how best to be yourself.

Parenting can be exhausting at times but there are days that will be better than others. I found having a newborn baby overwhelming, as doing many things, plus the addition of caring for a baby all at the same time was not easy.

Being a first-time mother meant I had to deal with feeling exhausted most of the time. During the birth of my daughter, I had an episiotomy performed. I experienced fascial tension, which was caused by the tear, and this meant I received stiches and experienced severe pelvic pain. My pelvic muscles were so weak, and it was difficult to walk, sit or stand for long periods of time. I learnt to take hot baths and practiced pelvic muscle exercise while in the bath, just to ease the sharpness of the pain.

Yes, you guessed it! Intimacy with my husband after childbirth was the last thing on my mind. I was too exhausted from doing housework and caring for my newborn baby. All my focus was on my beautiful baby girl. At the end of the day, all I wanted to do was get into my bed and sleep. I gave no thought to making myself attractive or even thinking about his needs. I felt like I was not in control of what I was experiencing. Breastfeeding was difficult as trying to make sure my baby latch on correctly left me swollen. I had so many mood swings: one minute, I felt like I was coping and the next minute, I was having thoughts of not being able to manage. This was not a good place to be. Therefore, it is important to be selfish sometimes, when it is something that is important to you.

Our health is important and most often, it is the one thing that we neglect the most. Often, we ignore the signs and messages our body is sending us. One of the key health problems we often ignore is post-natal depression. It is often put down to tiredness (baby blues) after the birth of a child. This is a common problem that affects lots of women within a year of giving birth. It doesn't just affect women after birth—it is known also to affect women during pregnancy.

So, what happen when you are unable to meet all these needs?

It was during one of these moments that I realised that I was not looking out for Number One (myself). My mother would say, "You have let yourself go," meaning I was not putting any effort into looking after myself. I started to spend time getting massages, having my hair done, and just pampering myself. This allowed me to feel good and receiving compliments for all the efforts I made was the difference required to enable me to build self-confidence and recharge my battery; it was just the medicine I needed.

I came to the place of understanding that self-care is not the opposite of compassion but the opposite of self-neglect. As a new mother, it is your job to ensure that you are not sacrificing yourself to serve others and putting others first. We should not neglect the messages our bodies indicate to tell us something needs their attention; it is important to prioritise and have boundaries.

Speaking to a first-time mum, this is what she shared. *"Being a parent is more challenging than I thought. The sleepless nights are the worst, the house is untidy, and the kitchen sink is always full of dishes. I just feel tired all the time."*

Like other first-time mothers, it can take a while to understand the importance of being a parent and looking after yourself. I know it took me awhile to understand that my health and wellbeing was just as important or even more so when there is another human being depending on you.

You can be a wonderful mum, taking care of the household and serving others, but if you do not look after yourself, you will end up being a wonderful, exhausted mum.

Giving time to yourself means paying attention to your body. This includes exercising, eating healthy and taking time for yourself even before childbirth. Schedule personal time and setup an evening with yourself. Book a night at the movies, or simple just go for a walk, get a manicure or massage. Taking care of yourself is part of loving your baby as well as loving yourself.

I was speaking to my friend (first-time parent) about being a parent, and she was expressing to me how difficult it was being a parent. She found it very challenging, and the worst part was the lack of sleep that had impacted negatively on her health.

You have to realise that you really can't give your best when you aren't at your best

You have to learn to first take care of yourself and make yourself a priority then you can take care of others.

Be intentional by first recognising that, as a mother, you also have needs. You need to take personal time to rest and take care of yourself. Do things that make you feel good and special. As a parent, our instinct is to focus on nurturing and helping our family and child. To cater to and take care of them. While it makes us feel good, it can be exhausting and drains us. If as a mother you do not take time to replenish yourself, you will end up resenting yourself for putting yourself last.

You want the very best for your child: every parent does. But as said before, raising a child can be overwhelming. There are health, safety, nutrition, self-esteem, education, and socialisation concerns. And that's just on a good day! And many parents even worry whether their child is growing and developing the way they should be.

Don't worry. Every parent has the same issues and worries. But sometimes you just need a little help. That's why I am committed to making things easier for parents of any age and experience.

Every child grows and develops differently, doing things at their own pace. However, children generally reach certain milestones in their lives at roughly the same time, so I have got several pages that describe each of the major age milestones, and what usually happens at that time. Understanding these will give you the chance to help your child develop new skills and reach their full potential.

These are mainly tips and practical advice that I have used, both with my own children or within the nursery setting, while working in partnership parents, caregivers and Early Years Practitioners that have proven successful.

"Parents are the First educators for their children."

As a parent, you are very influential as to how your child grows up and parent their own child. Most parents tend to communicate with their children the way their parent communicated, or not, with them as a child.

Three of the most important aspects of being a good role model for my children are:

1. The actions I display before my children sends a powerful message, so I am leading by example. As a parent, you should always keep in mind that your child is always watching you. That you are role model to your child and the behaviours that you display will be what your child will adopt. These behaviours will have a powerful impact on your child for the rest of their lives. Positive actions are the best tools that you can put in your child's toolkit on their journey of life. It creates habits in your child that will last a lifetime and transcend for generations to come. Your positive actions should include both your verbal and non-verbal communication.

2. Ensuring that there is open communication between my daughters and I. The key to getting it right is talking to your child and also listening to them without becoming judgemental or casting blame. Allow your child to know that it is okay to say "no" to their friends as well.

3. Allow your child to see that you also make mistakes. Being open and truthful to your child opens the door for them to come to you and tell you the truth, irrespective of what the situation is. It is the best foundation to build a parent and child relationship on.

It Sets expectations and Avoids Exploitation

This was true for me growing up in the Caribbean with my parents. My parents were clear in letting me know what they expected of my conduct. My dad would always remind me that it did not matter what the situation was, I should never lie to him. My father always reminded us to speak the truth at all times. He believed that if you had no knowledge of the truth, then it was not possible to effectively protect your child. Therefore, it was vital that we always spoke the truth, and our behaviour met his expectation.

Why is This Important

Our children need a good role model to teach them appropriate ways to build relationships. It also gives children an idea of what to expect. Role models act as a source of inspiration. My dad was my role model and he taught me to love and respect others. He also taught me that our actions, spoken words or nonverbal, has consequences. Children need to be taught from an early age about the basic ways to model behaviour and make decisions.

Growing up as a child, I understood non-verbal communication from my parents. If I displayed inappropriate behaviour, my parents would look at me. The non-verbal body language message would express that, my behaviour needed to change, so whatever I was doing, I needed to stop. The consequences would be clear when I got home. This did not mean that my home environment was not a happy one: far from it. It simply meant that there were boundaries that, as children, my siblings and I were not expected to cross.

If you were like me, you perhaps felt uncomfortable as a child when they displayed non-verbal communication, especially when out with my parents. As such, I learnt not to do the same with my children. I thought about how it made me feel and how I wanted my children to feel and the relationship I wanted to build with them.

My daughters feel comfortable to come and speak with me about any concerns they may be experiencing. I am able to help them to deal with peer pressure and other negative influences. My job as a parent is to set good examples and ensure that there are no barriers to communication. In doing so, I can ensure I am setting good communication, both verbal and non-verbal, communication.

Setting aside quality family time is important. Growing up, mealtimes were mainly the place for family discussions. It was a way for each family member to catch up on what was happening within the family. We could express any concerns and we were always encouraged to talk about our school day.

The message of Love

Smiling at your child conveys a message of love. from an early age, babies learn through their senses, so touching and stroking your baby's face sends the message that you love and care for them.

Body language plays an important part when speaking with your child. The more loving gestures you can give, the greater the bond and relationship you are building with your child.

Most importantly, tell your child "I love you" each and every day—many times throughout the day, in fact. When they've behaved badly, remind yourself that it's not them you don't like, only their behaviour. Put little sweet notes in their lunchboxes or coat pockets, or even send them a card in the mail. Soon, they'll learn to say "I love you" just as easily and honestly in return.

It's often been said that children learn what they live. So, if you're looking for a place to start helping your child understand the message of love, then let's show them love. Be positive when you speak about yourself and highlight your strengths. This will teach your child that it's okay to be proud of their talents, skills and abilities.

Turning away from your child when your child is seeking affection can cause your child to feel unloved and unworthy of being loved. Both positive expressions of love and verbal expressions of love is important in engaging with your child. This helps to build a relationship and build your child's self-esteem.

There are many lessons that my parents taught me that I continue to learn as a parent today. One of the most important lessons my parents taught me was to trust God, have faith and stay positive throughout hard times.

Some of the things I learnt in life, I have decided that I would not pass on to my children, and there is nothing wrong with that either.

As we grow up and society changes, we change along with it. So, we change the way we parent our children. The way I disciplined my first child is different from how I approached disciplining my two other children. The way you parent as the new generations come into the world, is totally different from how you were parented as a child. I am sure, like me, there are some good bits that you have decided to keep and some that you feel is time to throw out in the bath water. No parent is perfect but there are always things you can change to become better.

To be successful means to be consistent:

We tell our children to believe in themselves and that they can do anything if they set their minds to it. You want your child to believe in themselves and try their best, but as parents, we tell ourselves that some things are hard, we cannot do XYZ, or it is not going to work. My point is that it is okay to express to your child the challenges that you are experiencing. Allow your child to know that, at times, things can be difficult, but it does not mean you have thrown in the towel.

If you will not let your child believe they can fail, why are you telling yourself you are a failure?

Parents always worry about their children; it is in their nature.

To be successful simply means developing successful habits and sticking to them.

CHAPTER THREE: Understanding How Your Child Develops

"Imagine a world where every child comes with their own unique set of instructions."

Every parent wants the best for their children and for them to be happy, so that they can be engaging and reach their full potential. However, there are parents who do not know how to do this. Unless they are given the information, then they have no knowledge that they are missing vital information.

So, what is it that parents do not know that they do not know?

It is natural as a parent or a caregiver to worry about your child. Whether it is concern about their health, speech or how they are growing, parents will always have one concern or another. In a broader way, all these concerns can be summed up as child development. If you have no knowledge of what to do, then you are powerless to help your child.

No two children develop the same; however, there is an expectation of how children should develop. This is what we will look at and how, as parents, we can support our children to reach the expected milestone.

The overall development of your child will include the following aspects: their ability to learn or solve problems (brain functions) to form relations, dealing with their emotions, speaking using language (communicate), their ability to walk, using their limbs, hands and feet and their sensory skills, which include the ability to concentrate and follow instructions. These are the basic aspects of child development.

Building Relationship

As parents, we have the job of ensuring that we are supporting our children to meet these milestones. Children are naturally curious from birth; they are drawn to things. Once drawn, they want to explore and discover what, why and how, and this is the foundation of child development. As your child grows, they will go through different stages of development and processes. Some of these stages come naturally, while there are others that have to be taught. The key to growth and development is a parent's love and connection with their child.

Understanding your child means making connections, understanding how to communicate with your child from birth and being able to read your child's body language.

How do you go about doing that?

You start with the understanding that the first and most important part of parenting is connecting and building a relationship with your child. You can create bonds with your child through interactions. The time spent feeding and attending to your child's basic needs are special and can be used to bond over. The early stage of life requires a child to rely on the mother or caregiver for basic needs. The earlier, as a parent, we understand what is required of us, the sooner we can meet our child's need.

Learning On The Spot

As a first-time mother with little support, it took about two weeks to understand when my daughter needed to be comforted, from when she was hungry or required sleep.

I learnt to read my child's basic needs through the language of crying; I learnt to understand the different sounds my daughter made when she cried and that was my first step to understanding her.

Once I was able to understand the different sounds of my baby's cry, I found it easier to relate to her, knowing exactly what was happening her and was able to meet that need at a more effective pace. Knowing your child takes time, but it can be done.

I learnt that when I tickled my baby or touched and stroked her face, it was a form of stimulant that allowed her to respond. For example, I would sing a nursery rhyme and stop then she would make sounds. Bath time is one of the most favourite times to connect with your baby. Too often when we grow up and become parents, we forget how to be playful, but our babies can teach us so many things. If we can get out of the way of our egos, we will be alright.

Playing with your child from birth is the most important aspect of their development. Smiling and talking to your child supports their development. It is during these precious moments that a parent will become aware of any concerns about their child's development.

Understanding your child means making connections, understanding how to communicate with them from birth and being able to read your child's body language.

The Best Foundation for Life

For every parent, the experience of childbirth is different. Some parents feel an intense attachment within the first minutes or days after birth. For others, it may take a bit longer. Bonding is a process, not something that takes place within minutes and not something that has to be limited to happening within a certain time period after birth. This is important for both mums and dads.

Bonding and being close enables a child to feel secure and affects how they will interact, communicate and form relationships later in life. The bond you develop is a key factor in the way your baby's brain develops and influences their social, emotional, intellectual, and physical development.

Even before birth, your baby can recognise sounds. In the first days of life, your baby picks up on your cues, your tone of voice, your gestures, and your emotions and sends you signals by crying, cooing, mimicking facial expressions, and eventually smiling, laughing, pointing, and even yelling. In return, you watch and listen to your baby's cries and sounds, and respond to their cues, at the same time as you tend to their need for food, warmth, and affection. The nurturing your baby receives in the first days and weeks helps to form a bond with you. A secure attachment grows out of the success of this bonding process between you and your baby. Every stroke, smile and touch you give to your new-born baby allows them to learn about who you are and life.

You connect to your new-born baby by paying attention to the kinds of movements, sounds, and environments your baby enjoys. Some babies are comforted by motion, such as rocking or being walked back and forth, while others respond to sounds like soft music, or a change of environment such as being carried outside. Most of your baby's early signs and signals are about their need for comfort, food, and sleep.

Play and Fun

Having fun, playing with, holding, and sharing happiness with your baby is really important. Smiles, laughter, touch, and interaction are important to a baby's development. Your body language, tone of voice, and loving touch are all ways of communicating with your baby.

Watch your baby's facial expressions and body movements for clues about their needs. For example, your baby may adjust body position or facial expression, or move their arms and legs in response to your voice or to tell you they are cold and need to be cuddled. Become familiar with the kinds of sounds your baby makes and what these sounds mean.

When you see signs that your baby wants to play, try to relax and enjoy exchanging smiles, funny faces, and silly sounds with your child. Toys, books, and music can provide a helpful starting point for play, but often, all it takes is a game of peek-a-boo or a silly voice to invite your baby to play. Your local Children's Centre may run activities, such as baby massage, that can support bonding with your baby. Enjoy reading and sharing books together or join a baby and toddler group.

Creating an environment that supports your child development

As your child grows and develop, they will start to explore their environment. Being active means your child's gross motor skills are developing. The muscles needed to run, jump and walk upstairs need to be strong. Playing is a great way to energise and teach your child. For example, you can count the steps as you go up and down the stairs. As you build your relationship with your child through play, story time and song time, the best part of this relationship is you.

As a parent, you play the biggest role in your child's development by engaging with your child and using their interest as your starting point. You are the first person that can educate your child and effectively support your child in building their independent skills. Meeting your child at their level will nurture and strengthen bonds and connection with you. Not only are children learning to explore their environment, but they are also learning to navigate rules in their world.

- Support your toddler's attempts to be more independent.
- Allow your child to develop a sense of mastery.
- Set limits to ensure their safety and your well-being.
- Show that you tolerate his or her anger and other emotions.
- Try to see things from your toddler's perspective.
- Keep your child safe during their explorations.
- Encourage his or her curiosity.

No matter what age or stage of development your child is at, it is never too early to set boundaries for them.

Setting boundaries

What are they?

Boundaries are rules that we put in place for safety purposes.

As parents, our role is to look after our children, and this includes keeping them safe. One of the biggest reasons for setting boundaries is so as not to waste your "me time," have sleepless nights and become overwhelmed doing everything for your child.

Keeping them safe means setting boundaries and putting routines in place within the home. One of the earliest boundaries parents set is around safety guidelines. You don't want to be the parent that says "NO" to your toddler all day long. You want to be a positive parent who can say "no" by setting boundaries for your toddler without being negative.

Every day we live our lives by expectations and rules that we put in place to maintain stability. As parents and adults, we put rules in place for our children, around behaviour and safety, to ensure that they can maintain and interact with others appropriately.

One of the main reason for having boundaries, is for when your little one discovers the word "no" you are able to be firm and consistency in giving instructions. Something that is simple and easy for them to follow. Boundaries are the safety net that allows your child to explore but within reason.

It is everything from your child throwing a tantrum in the supermarket to throwing all their dinner on the floor. From them hitting or biting others, to learning turn taking.

Setting routine and boundaries both for yourself as well as your child is one of the most important part of parenting you can ever do. Yes, I agree with you that it is exhausting but if you are a parent, caregiver or work with children, setting boundaries is part and parcel of raising children.

Your child will always be looking to testing any boundaries, until they come to the point of realisation that you are irremovable, and they are not getting anywhere.

TIPS FOR SUCCESS BOUNDARIES FOR TODDLERS

- Decide on what boundary you want to set before your toddler is throwing a tantrum.

- Do not put too many boundaries in at once: for a toddler, a maximum of three at a time is good.

- Use clear and simple words that your toddler can follow - simple instructions.

- Be clear and consistent in the boundaries you set.

- Be gentle and firm using a calm voice. Do not allow your emotions to get the better of you.

- Distract your child by offering an alternative, so they shift their focus.

- If your child is energetic by nature, give your child something to channel that energy into that they enjoy doing.

- Boundaries work well when all parties agree.

- Your job is to teach your child what is acceptable behaviour, when you see them doing something that is totally unacceptable.

CHAPTER FOUR: Being an Effective Parent

In a nutshell, to me, being an effective parent means to be able to engage with your child in a way that supports them developing the knowledge and emotional skills to become happy and productive adults and have well-adapted behaviours.

To be a success in this competitive world, therefore, we must teach our children how to be honest and have self-control. They must be able to make decisions and function independently yet be kind and empathetic to others. They need to know how to cooperate with others, form relationship based on healthy moral principles and behave appropriately, even in difficult circumstances.

Why is parenting important?

Parenting is an important part of loving and caring for your child. Good parenting is about providing a warm, secure home life. The overall development of your child will include their ability to learn or solve problems, form relationship and deal with their emotions.

As parents, we have the job of ensuring that we are supporting our children to learn the rules of life (e.g., how to share, respecting others, etc.) and to self-regulate (deal with their emotions).

You may have to stop them from doing things they should not be doing, but it is just as important to encourage them to do the things you do want them to do.

Parenting is never easy; in fact, it is one of the most challenging and often frustrating yet most rewarding thing you will ever do, especially since all parents are learning as they go. No parent goes into parenting knowing exactly what to expect, or how to handle every situation that will arise. But the best parents are the ones who are always looking for ways to improve their parenting skills.

Setting limits (boundaries) are an important part of everyday life. It gives children a better outcome when they know what to expect and what is expected of them. It supports their emotional and mental health, thus allowing children to have the skills they need to overcome challenges and difficulties they will face during life. It will help them to be able to make decisions with positive outcomes we can be proud off.

From an early age, it is important to teach children the importance of showing respect and how to demonstrate appropriate behaviour, to ensure they are able to form relationships.

What helps?

It is important to make sure that children feel secure, loved and valued, and that all adults looking after them notice when they are behaving well. The trick to this is to find strategies that work well for you and your child.

Here are some ideas:

* Be consistent

When starting something new with your child, it is important to be consistent. Children like to have consistency; it gives them a sense of belonging and helps them to know what is expected.

Often, as parents we struggle to not give into the demands of our children. We feel that if we do not give into our children, they will not love us anymore.

Try to say the same thing each time and be clear about the rules you want to stick to. If you do not stick to the rules and give in, then the next time you try to set limits, your child is likely to play up even more because they have learned that you will probably give in. Consistency is important, irrespective of age. As parents, we are positioned to demonstrate what is required, to be able to ensure there is consistency in the way we care for our children. Depending on the age of your child, you may be able to sit down and talk with them about good behaviour. You might be surprised about how much you both agree on.

* Give lots of praise

Let your children know when they have done something well and when you are pleased with them. Be specific so that the child knows which behaviour you are wanting to encourage. For example, give them a hug or a kiss, tell them how great they are doing, and point out the good behaviour. You need to do this straightaway at the time when you see the behaviour you want to encourage.

* Planning ahead

It helps if you and your child know the rules for particular situations before they happen. Do not make them up as you go along (e.g., if bedtime is 7.00 p.m., make sure you both stick to it).

* Be calm

This can be difficult in the heat of the moment, but it does help if you can be calm and clear with the words you use. For example, "Please switch off the TV." or "It's bedtime."

* Be clear with your child

For example, "Please put your toys away" tells your child exactly what you want them to do. Simply telling them to "be good" will not help them to know what behaviour you are expecting. If your child cannot understand you, they cannot co-operate with you; therefore, it is best to keep instructions brief and positive.

* Be realistic

It's no good promising a wonderful reward or threatening to remove their favourite activity if you cannot keep your word. It is much better to offer small rewards rather than punishments. For example, "When you have tidied your room, you can go to the park." Don't expect too much too soon as change usually takes time. For this reason, expect your child to progress in small steps. So, if your child has started to or partly tidied their room, praise them for what they have done. You can say, "Well done for putting those toys in the box." * The importance of your relationship that you are building with your child is the foundation that you are setting to support your child making relations as they grow.

As your child develops from a baby and toddler to primary school age and teenager, many things change but basic principles remain the same. As an awesome parent, you will balance his or her maturity level and needs with rules, responsibilities, and allowances.

While the younger child is more self-centred and less understanding of others' expectations, the teenager is more attuned to compromise, negotiation, and developing their independence and identity.

Knowing how to be a good parent is intuitive. Trust and follow your instinct. Gauge and act according to your child's display of maturity.

* Create structure

Communicate often and openly. Listen attentively. Encourage your children to talk about their experiences and emotions.

Demonstrate empathy and trust.

Most of all, enjoy your children at whatever age they are. It is a time of learning and sharing, reaching new heights together. Be there while they grow.

My parenting advice of how to connect with your child so that they realise their full potential is to start by being open, listen and give your child your full attention. Allowing your child to finish what they are saying before responding is just as important. Another way you can do that is to teach your child to say "thank you" to other people. The earlier a child learns that manners go a long way, the sooner the child will come to understand respecting adults is part of growing up.

This is just as vital as encouraging your child to express gratitude to you. You deserve it, after all, even though many parents view the hard work they do to raise their child/children as simply part of the job. By doing this, we are undoing the message to children that it's important to give as well as accept.

Chapter Five: Values Are For Life

Teaching children good, moral values and respect builds your child's character. Being able to say "sorry," having humility, being kind to friends, learning to share and turn taking, forms the core of their being and is the foundation of their moral belief. It is important that children are taught these values from an early age.

Values are important beliefs shared by the members of a culture or family about what is good and what is not. It wields major influence on the behaviour of an individual and serve as rules or guidelines in all situations. Some fundamental moral values are honesty, respect, integrity and responsibility.

It is important to teach children to conduct themselves in ways that allow them to develop gratifying relationships with other people and to build their self-esteem. This will improve a child's view of themselves whilst, at the same time, develop their self-confidence and self-worth. These are skills that as parents we need to include in their development. The way your children will learn values is by observing what you are doing and drawing a conclusion about things you think are important in life.

Teaching children ethics and good values help to build their character, help them to know the difference between right and wrong, change their perception of the world, support them in making decisions and help ensure they are not easily influenced by others. Children who feel good about themselves are less likely to follow certain trends and are more able to cope with difficult situations.

Parents are best placed to support and encourage their children to take challenges and learn from making mistakes. Your role as a parent, caregiver or early years practitioner is to offer guidance and not take over or interfere with what your child is doing. Allow your child time to figure things out for his or herself.

As parents, we will only understand how much our children know when we give them space to come up with their own solutions to the problem. The best way to do that is to create an environment where your child feels secure and loved and they are truly supported to achieve.

Children do not like to be pushed into situations that are out of their comfort zone. Support your child to extend their ideas through discussion by asking open-ended questions that allow your child to think "how" and "why" things happen. Give them time and space to think through situations and come to conclusions independently. Irrespective of whether they are right or wrong, the skills you are teaching your child is to think.

Allow your child to know that it is okay to make a mistake, as being able to make mistakes is a massive learning curve for your child. It is behooved to parents to teach their children social values.

Teach your child to make positive choices, and praise them for good deeds, good behaviours and positive attitudes they possess. Encourage them to become actively involved in their community and introduce them to activities that promote a sense of cooperation and accomplishment. Be firm yet fair when handing down discipline for misdeeds or misbehaviours. Make certain the rules and consequences for breaking the rules are clearly defined. Show a cooperative, loving and united front with your spouse when it comes to discipline.

In today's society, the parenting focus has shifted to a more child-centred rearing method. Gone are the days when children are disciplined for any wrongdoings. As a result, children today are often let off the hook and are rarely held accountable for their actions. They are not guided into taking responsibility for their actions. They are not consistently taught right from wrong, and it is the responsibility of every parent to teach their child these values.

Raising children is more challenging than ever and shaping children's character is even more urgent as children are confronted daily with values that seem to oppose their parents' values. There are mixed messages through media, other adults and peers about core values and ethics.

In today's society, children find it much harder to learn basic lessons of self-management, self-esteem and empathy towards others.

Train Them to Be Accountable

In spite of these challenges, parents are still the best protection against children participating in risky behaviour that show a lack of moral standards, lack of self-esteem and empathy towards others.

Parents are responsible for preparing their children for adult life. Teach them that if they want something, effort should be exerted in order to achieve it. Money is not the important thing; being responsible and independent is what matters. Provide them their allowance for jobs but don't pay them if they are not doing their part. This way, you are preparing them to survive in this world.

Building Self-esteem

It's often been said that children learn what they live. So, if you're looking for a place to start helping your child build positive self-esteem and self-value, then you should show them your positive sense of self and strong self-esteem. Be positive when you speak about yourself and highlight your strengths. This will teach your child that it's okay to be proud of their talents, skills and abilities. When children are given opportunity to do good things, it allows them to feel good about themselves.

They learn how to care and respect when they are treated with care and respect. When they feel love, they become more attached and more receptive to moral values and ethics.

Your child also benefits greatly from honest and positive praise. Find something about them to praise each day. You could even give your child a task you know they can complete and then praise them for a job well done after they're finished. This will demonstrate to your child that positive acts merit positive praise; doing this helps to develop a sense of belonging. Loving, nurturing relationships are sustained through the bond you develop with your children. It allows them to develop a real sense of who they are, and a sense of belonging. Love is the foundation on which every aspect of your relationship with your child should be built on. Children need to be rooted and grounded in love as this helps them to develop positive self-concept and a sense of worth. This type of parenting love looks like focused attention, time, support boundaries and commitment.

Having a Sense of Belonging

Children need to develop the skills for forming stable and affectionate relationships and maintaining these from an early age with others. They need to develop self-awareness of their needs as well as the need of others. Supportive parents help their children to develop as capable and competent persons who can stand up for what is right, without needing the approval of their peers.

One way to support your child's self-awareness is to start with ensuring your child feels secure in their environment, feels loved and have a sense of belonging.

When your child can identify things that belong to him or her, they are learning about identity. As young as twelve months, a child will start to speak, and you will hear words like "mine": this is the start of a child taking ownership. Start by allowing your child to learn to put away their toys. Labeling items is another way of developing their communication skills as they are being taught how to identify where things go.

Teaching children how to develop a sense of belonging can be as simple as being able to identify their coat peg in a nursery setting. Having a child's picture on their coat peg gives that child a sense that they are part of that environment, and for them to make sense of the world.

Being able to make friends and identify who their friends are is another way to help children develop a sense of belonging.

A child going off to nursery for the first time can be very frightening for them. Parents can help by speaking to their child in preparation of what to expect. Having to deal with new surroundings and new faces can be frightening. Reassure your child by speaking to them about starting nursery or school. Explain to your child about what to expect, routine, the breakdown of the day, etc.

Takes a Village to raise a child

Growing up in a little village in Jamaica, I was raised by the entire community, meaning, the people in the community looked out for my well-being alongside my immediate family. If it was discipline that needed to be instilled in me then it was the role of any member of the community to highlight the aspect of my behaviour that was unacceptable and set in motion ways that I could change. To be disrespectful to an adult was unacceptable behaviour from a child.

In today's on-the-go society, our community is different; we hardly know who our neighbours are or what they do. We are so busy carving out life for ourselves that we don't have any time to get to know our neighbours. Life has changed and this is not just in big cities but in rural communities as well. I grew up with the freedom as a child to play outside with friends, without my parents being present. This was acceptable as other members of the community were present to look out for us. Today, this is frowned upon and seen as a safeguarding concern.

Liz's Story:

This is an account of an incident that my friend, Liz, encountered whilst shopping in a famous store in London. *Out shopping, I took the escalator up a floor and as I was about to get off, there was a child looking very upset and on the verge of tears. I said, "Hi, are you okay?" He looked around and I didn't know what to do. I looked around and couldn't see who he was supposed to be with. I asked him, "Have you lost your mummy and daddy?" He nodded his head in response and at that point, I started to panic a little and started thinking to myself what I should do and if I should hold his hand. Unsure of what to do, I raised my voice a little louder and again asked, "Are you looking for your mummy and daddy?"*

Just then, I saw someone in a cubicle across from where I was. They were talking about furniture with the salesperson, and they waved at the child, and he went towards them.

This new society of today that we live in shows people are fearful of approaching children.

When they see a child in distress, they are fearful that the child may get the wrong idea of their motive as children are being taught about stranger danger. At first, the child may not have realised that the adult is coming to help as, until that adult has an opportunity to reassure the child that they want to help, it's a 50/50 chance.

Adults are fearful of approaching a child to give support as they too are fearful that others may come to the wrong conclusion of their motives. This can lead to an array of things like confrontation, accusation and miscommunication.

Liz went from, "what do I do?" because you are not allowed to approach children and not allowed to touch children to "what if someone sees me talking to a child, I have no connection with?" The fact that the child was close to the escalator peaked her concern as a safety issue first.

Often, when children are separated from their parents, it can be a very distressing feeling. For the child, this could have caused him massive stress, especially since this situation could have gone wrong in so many different ways.

In most cases, children are not given an opportunity to express how they feel or speak about their emotions. This would have given them an opportunity for the child to talk about how he felt when he could not see his parents, etc. This is vital when parents separate, or they have lost a loved one. Corporate parenting can help children to make sense of what is happening. It is about building an identity that allows the child to understand that they are part of something special which involves a wider community.

CHAPTER SIX: A critical and engaging child

Critical thinking starts with us as adults; it is how we interpret what is being said to us and how we learn from interpreting and experiencing the world around us. It means to be able to process information and shows that we are open to new ideas.

Adults must first have an awareness of this skill, to be able to apply it in parenting.

Critical thinking is also considered as giving children the tools that help them to develop the skills for reasoning, analyzing, comparing and contrasting so they can succeed in everyday life. It relates to skills children need in connecting pieces of information for effective communication.

It can be seen as a way in which children take the lead with contributions from adults (practitioner, parent) to build on their knowledge, in an environment where the adult does not control the process but supports the process.

Using the curiosity approach to teach children how to become critical thinkers may seem daunting at first, but it is an essential skill that children need to develop. There are simple techniques that can be used to explain critical thinking to children so that they are able to interpret what is happening in this fast-paced world.

Ways To Support Children

One way we can support their critical thinking is reading aloud to our children. Reading books to children stimulates their imagination and creativity. This will expand their understanding of the world, develop their cognitive development and skill, whilst improving their understanding of the written word. Cognitive development is the emergence of the ability to think and understand; it is the construction of the thought process.

It helps them to develop their language and communication skills; as we read aloud, children are learning new words and are developing their vocabulary. Therefore, the more they know, the more they understand about the world and perception of things.

Communication and language open the door to your child's learning ability. You can help your child develop their communication skills through listening. The possibilities are endless when children are given opportunities to express themselves using language and different kinds of words.

The most important is not the number of words your child hears, but the number of different words. The wider your child's vocabulary is expanded, the greater their usage of words.

Repetition is key to engagement. Talking in a clear, calm voice to your child brings emphasis to the conversation. But always following your child's lead is paramount.

Reading aloud also helps to develop their listening skills, as children are able to participate in the story and can give their input into the story. One way of knowing if the child is listening is asking questions about the story, to gain awareness if the child is following the story. Doing this will improve their concentration and memory.

Another reason why adults should read aloud to their child is that reading develops a special bond with the child. Over time, your child will learn to look forward to that special time together. Your child will trust and expect that special bond that comes from parent-child relationship or between a child and caregiver.

It helps children to reason through important decisions, solve problems, generate creative ideas and set goals—all of which are necessary for future developing. Children should be given the opportunity to draw on their knowledge and existing experience or to use problem-solving skills and engage in the day-to-day activities.

Adults should always be looking at ways to enhance these abilities in children of all ages. Giving them opportunities to be able to compare and contrast, to explain why things happen and evaluate ideas from opinion, for them to be able to come to a conclusion or form judgement.

This enables children to think critically and rationally and encourages looking for alternative ways to solve a problem.

This is an essential life skill, and we all need to have a critical thinking mindset which makes solving everyday problems easier. There are many ways we can engage children to become critical thinkers. Children are born with a curious mind: they want to know why things happen, how things work etc.

Parents, caregivers and Early Years Practitioners are best placed to develop children's curiosity. The most effective way to support a child's critical thinking is by using fun, educational games and activities that help children to become critical thinkers. It can be Early Years Practitioners setting out activities that are open ending that allow children to use resources to create ideas that they can build on. You can read to children and give them opportunities to ask the right questions and figure out how and why things are the way they are.

How to Teach your kids to become Critical Thinkers

Practitioners, parents and caregivers need to build critical thinking in children through daily interactions, talking with children, asking open-ended questions, allowing children to experiment and problem solving.

Children are full of questions, aren't they? So, to encourage their thinking process, you can ask them to try answering their questions. And in the process, you can help them arrive at the answer using logic process, instead of providing them with a direct answer. Children need to be able to process the *who*, *why* and *what* questions by being given the appropriate time and space to do so.

Children learn from observing the adult they are with, how the adult navigate problems and deal with situations they face daily. This plays an integral part in how children develop their critical thinking skills.

Some children struggle with critical thinking, but this is where the adult (practitioner) can intervene and use a practical example. They can verbalize what the child is doing and how the child thinks.

One great way to connect with your child is to do activities with them. For example, depending on your child's age, have fun baking a cake. Help your child to talk about the ingredients needed to bake a cake. Shop together for the ingredients. Allow your child to make a **shopping list** and even encourage them to write the list. It may not be legible, so ask your child to name the items on the list. You can discuss what item can be found where and the number of the aisle. Build your child's vocabulary by repeating words that are not pronounced correctly.

Discuss your child's interests as you interact throughout the day. It's very helpful to repeat a word in more than one situation. When you repeat a word many times, in different situations, you give your child lots of opportunities to understand the word and eventually use it on his own! As you actively listen to your child and support your child with ideas for logical thinking, you are helping your child by giving them the building blocks for learning.

"Because I say so" Just doesn't Work (or isn't the answer)

Remember that children are inquisitive by nature. When they are young, they ask questions because they usually want to better understand something. When they are older, it's because they want to better understand why you think something is important and why they should also feel the same way. Regardless of their age, it's imperative that children are given opportunities to reason and come to their own conclusion about how, and why things are the way they are.

Sometimes the best way to teach your kids an important life skill is to model it in your own life. After all, kids tend to copy the behaviours they see in their parents.

When you encourage your child from an early age to engage in critical thinking that leads into open communication, it allows them to understand that their thoughts, feelings and opinions have value. What they say matters to you.

Parenting is about engaging with your child. Your child will learn more when you engage them in everyday activities based on their curiosity and interest.

Finding out what your child likes and what their interests are starts with talking to them, paying attention to what makes them happy and knowing what your child likes to spend time doing. You should find out what your child's favourite toy is and what they like to play with. Once you are aware of what your child likes to do, that's your starting place.

How to Discover Your Child's Interests

The first step to finding out your child's interest is by spending time with them. Observe and show an interest by talking to your child. While you might know many of your child's interests, taking a closer look might give you some new information. The next step in using this information is to build communication through observation.

In order to observe a child's interest, you need to meet at their level.

Getting down to your child's level might include lying on the floor with your child while your child is playing with cars, or trains, etc. Be face to face with them, giving them your full attention while you are engaging. Follow your child's lead; allow your child to show and tell you what they are doing.

If you notice that your child likes spending time building things, feed that interest. Look out for what makes your child laugh and keeps them engaged.

Using a child's interests and everyday activities provides so many more learning opportunities. A child whose interest is dinosaurs can be used to engage the child in other aspects of learning around that scope of things. The idea is to provide the child with as much learning opportunities as possible.

Within the home environment, a vast number of learning opportunities are available. You can use these opportunities to develop your child's independent skills. If your child likes to cook, why not develop some special recipes of what your child likes to eat and help them in preparing a meal.

Working with children, I have learnt to observe children and to be able to say what each child likes to do. For example, if your child loves music, teach your child by using instruments, songs, rhythms and actions. You can teach your child to spell their name by using two or three beats using their favourite nursery rhythms song. Teaching them colours, names, alphabet, season, is also possible. The list is endless.

A child can be taught through their interest how to recognise size, shape, position and use language to express their feelings through playing with a train, for example.

Another child is taught to count, recognise numbers, sorting different shapes or colour of cars. A child can be taught how to group things, depending on their age.

Create opportunities to use the interest in trains for learning turn taking and pretend play. This can include a trip to a train station, visit to a museum to look at earliest model of trains, etc. Use language to interject and interact about trains. Talk to your child about different modes of transportation. Asking open-ending questions will support engaging and showing an interest in these activities.

Listening to Your Child

Listening to your child holds a lot of importance, as it helps your child build a bond with you and develop their relationship and confidence. Active listening takes skills that are developed over time.

Actively listening means focusing on what your child is saying. This way, you will be able to pick up on what keeps them happy and engaged. At Nursery, we have what is called the twelve-second rule. When a child is asked a question, it takes twelve seconds for the child to understand and interpret what they are being asked.

Active listening means being aware of the tone of your voice when asking a question. Your body language and the message you are conveying to your child are all very important.

While some children are naturally expressive, some aren't.

Start by being open to listening and giving your child your full attention. Allow your child to finish what they are saying before responding in a sensitive manner, using language that your child can understand.

When you listen to your child, you get to know what they are thinking, feeling and going through.

Good communication is also a key to understanding your child better. Do not be surprised at how your child could be. These days, children know how to use misbehaviour and annoying habits just to raise parents up. It is not good to declare an all-out war with your child. Instead, it is always best to build and maintain a harmonious relationship to keep the parent and child relationship healthy and flourishing.

Here are some steps to incorporate into how you could better understand and control your child. It is not effective to be always ill-tempered and impulsive.

First, be genuinely familiar with the language used by the child, especially during times of conflicts and confrontations. Try your best to familiarise yourself with your child's accent, choice of words, and diction. Try to understand that as an individual, your child will eventually acquire and use their own speaking style. Being familiar with their own language can enable you to accurately decipher the message. Keep in mind that some children may not be knowledgeable or able to express real thoughts and emotions.

Second, learn how to accept the full emotional range of your child. Try to learn how to accept the emotions and feelings of your child, especially when they speak. As you succeed in understanding your child and their emotions, you may start guiding them to effectively express unpleasant and unlikely feelings in an acceptable and appropriate way. Do not discourage them from saying what they really feel. Suppression of emotions and feelings, as you know, is not healthy in the long-term.

Third, do not interrupt your child whenever they speak. It is good if you would actually show them the proper courtesy as they should to other people. As they speak, let them finish; this will show that interrupting any speaker is rude. This is also a way of instilling some parts of good values.

Fourth, always strive to be approachable. As much as possible, your child should not grow distant from you. If you are approachable enough, they will not hesitate to approach you to discuss any problem or request. Do not make your child feel and think as if communication is hard. It is advisable that the child realises that good and open communication between the both of you is always possible. Whenever they communicate, do not make them feel avoided, ignored or neglected.

Fifth, ask questions so you can gather further information. It is always advisable to ask good and light questions, especially if you are confirming your thoughts. However, try not to sound as interrogating and as intimidating as possible. Try to ask questions that could really solicit honest and direct answers from your child. Do not scare or annoy them through any of your inquisitions. Always observe a kind and pleasant manner so you can help your child bolster their self-esteem and confidence.

Lastly, provide good, helpful and assuring responses or answers to your child's every question. It would be helpful if you would apply reflective listening. This way, you can have a clear and actual grasp of what it is your child is trying to tell you. Reflect on the child's words and the manner in which the child talks. You could get a lot of clues and answers from them. Understanding your child entails setting good and open communication between you and them as part of preparation for life.

Building Blocks For Learning

1. As a parent, you play the biggest role in your child's development. By engaging with your child, use their curiosity and interest as your starting point. You are the first person that can educate your child and effectively support your child in building independent skills.

2. Meeting your child at their level will give them the advantage of nurturing and strengthen bonds and connection with you.

You can share by listening to what your child has to say and help by asking open-ended questions.

3. Focus on your child when spending time and use as many different activities as possible to give your child the building blocks to put words together and develop language.

4. Engage with your child by doing activities with them. This can be from reading, baking or drawing. The possibilities are endless in terms of the ways you can show an interest in what your child is interested in doing, so get involved, don't forget to have fun and smile to let your child see that you are enjoying yourself. Keeping your child healthy is one of the most important aspects of parenting.

CHAPTER SEVEN: How Much is Healthy?

Health deals with and plays an important part in all areas of our lives, including the physical, emotional, spiritual and physiology aspects of our well-being. The health of your child is one of the biggest concerns a mother will ever have. Adults' own attitude towards food often stem from our cultural influences, traditions and, as adults, our own childhood experiences and environments. This will result in the type of food we feed our children.

Therefore, we must teach our children healthy habits. This often starts with parents rethinking their own perception of what healthy habits are.

Diet and nutrition are key factors in the health and growth of a child. Children require lots of nutrients to help their bodies develop all the necessary functions and tissues they need, and the quality (or lack thereof) of these nutrients can have a big impact on their health.

Children's food intake patterns can be influenced by adults or role models around them and the diet a child has. It has an influence on everything, from basic brain functions to behavioural problems or even a child's aptitude to concentrate and have social interaction with others.

Nutrition is also involved in the prevention of many childhood diseases, especially conditions like obesity and diabetes, which affect a large percentage of children in today's society.

Help Your Child Stay Healthy for Life

Yes, it's true! The first years set the stage for healthy habits that mirrors the entire life of your child. We know how significant the first years are for getting your child off to a healthy start. We also understand that being a parent is an important—and hard—job! **Adults are the influencers, so it is crucial that they support the children growing up happy and healthy.**

I believe that no parent deliberately encourages their children to have a diet high in sugar, unhealthy fats, and salts. The difficulties are that many parents are now aware that toddlers' nutritional needs are quite different from older children and adults.

Involving Everyone

- Whether you are a parent, grandparent, early years professional or teacher, children look up to us and follow by example. They naturally imitate adults' behaviour in their process of growth, so it's crucial that we make the most of this time to encourage good eating habits.

- This puts a lot of responsibility on all of us as adults. It may seem impossible to be on our best behaviour all the time, especially as a practitioner or parent, but trying not to eat

unhealthy foods or snack when children are in the vicinity will encourage healthier eating habits.
- On average, a large percentage of children's early experiences with food are shaped by the behaviours and feeding practices of the caregiver.

My early childhood food experience was shaped, to a large degree, by the cultural food I was given. For example, I ate seasonal food that my father had grown on the farm, so there would be an abundance of that item on the dinner table for as long as the crop lasted. My mother learnt to use the food items in diverse ways in a variety of dishes. I dear to say not always to our liking; however, we knew that we had no choice but to eat what was prepared.

In the past, parents/families had to cope with food scarcity. Some hard-working families even today struggle to put food on their tables or provide a balanced meal for their children. A lack of food nutritional knowledge meant children were given any food item that was available, without any thought of the nutrient value.

Today, we have a different problem with food and its intake; there has been a shift from children being given meals prepared from fresh food produce to ready-made meals that are energy dense and low in nutrients. This has impacted some of our children's behaviours, emotions, functional abilities, and health due to the modification of natural foods to meet demands. We have an abundance of food and little time to prepare a balanced meal for our children and families. Fast Food is on the increase as more families are eating on the go. Children are coming home to an empty house and are left to prepare microwaveable dinners for themselves, which is then consumed in their bedrooms. Families no longer sit down to family mealtime, spend time at the dinner table or share their day's experience and this has led to a breakdown in family values, communication, and family perceptions of health.

Dos and *Don'ts* When It Comes to Your Child's Diet

- What if you only consider eating carrots?
- Do you think it would be healthy to only eat chocolate?

Food contains nutrients, and it is important that both adults and children eat a variety of food from all the food groups and not just from a particular group.

Eating a healthy diet means that the food we consume gives our bodies all sort of nutrients our bodies require for it to function properly. Children of different ages require distinct levels of nutrition; this is why adults should strive on creating a harmonic relationship between food and children. Some of the foods that contain the best nutrients in high proportion include:

- **Fruit:** Nearly all types of fruits are great for healthily adding nutrients to your diet. Make sure to target fruits without added sugars—canned fruits or fruit juices often have a lot of these additives, so it's essential to read nutrition labels when choosing what to buy at the grocery store.

- **Vegetables:** Veggies are bit of a hassle for kids to eat, but they're just as important as fruits. Be cautious of frozen or canned veggies because they can sometimes be very high in sodium. Look for a variety of colours in veggies, as these can represent various nutrients that our body demands i.e., broccoli, and other green leafy vegetables.
- **Protein:** Lean meats and poultry, plus things like beans, eggs, nuts, and various soy products, are good. Make sure, however, to maintain proper portion sizes with protein.
- **Dairy:** Look for low-fat dairy products whenever possible, or even better, soy-based dairy products.
- **Grains:** Look for whole grains over refined grains.

Foods to Avoid

Foods that contain fewer nutrients, or that might contain bad elements for your child's health, include:

- **Sugar and sweets:** This refers to added and processed sugars, not the kind naturally found in fruit. Consuming too much of these sugars is often a primary cause of diabetes.
- **Fats:** Avoid saturated and trans fats often found in red meats and full-fat dairy. Lots of oily, fatty foods contain these bad fats, and they can cause high blood pressure, cholesterol, and heart conditions.
- Giving children fizzy drinks and sugary sweet cakes are bad for children's health. It ruins their teeth and cause your child to lack energy.
- Never put children to bed with sugary drinks, this can lead to tooth decay.

The quickest and easiest way to remember how to make good food choices is by using the food traffic light system. Where green represents food with the highest value that our body needs to go and grow.

Food from the yellow group is food we can eat daily but we should limit the amount eaten from this group. While they can still be healthy and okay to eat daily, the portion should be kept in the correct portion. These includes, pasta, crackers, bread, cheese, eggs nuts, chicken, and other foods in this group.

Red Light Means Stop!

These are food you need to stop and think about before eating.

- Is there a better choice?
- Is there an alternative?
- Try not to eat too much from this group.
- Yes, they are yummy, for example, cookies, biscuits, pastries, chips, candies, sugary foods.
- They cause our body to feel full and release quick energy, but the energy goes away real fast...
- They make the body feel tired and cause the body to lack concentration skills.
- When we eat too much 'red-light food' and not enough green and yellow light food, it makes our bodies feel sick, and does not give us the nutrients to work, play or grow.

- Red-light foods should be eaten in moderation, as they give the body the least amount of nutrients.
- For most parents, getting their child to eat from the green group can be a hassle. When vegetables are not introduced at an early age, oftentimes children grow up refusing to eat their vegetables.

Did you know that what we eat also impacts the way we feel? Research from **The Denby Report** (2013) by Nigel Denby has shown that 65% of the salt in the UK diet comes from processed and convenience foods, not from the salt that is added at the dinner table or during the cooking process. This is a great contributor of high blood pressure, heart disease and stroke. While too much sugar in our diet can lead to weight gain, and fatty liver disease.

To give our children the best chance is to feed them the nutrients that will support their body to grow and develop. Another key factor to bear in mind is that a child-size portion of food is smaller than an adult size. Children should be given child-size meals at all times.

SIZE PORTIONS

- Keeping in mind that not all children are fussy eaters, some children are going to enjoy their meals. As with anything, knowing the right amount to feed a child during mealtime comes with practice.
- If you're not sure of what a child's meal portion size should be, or what food is best for their child, a good place to start is by using our hand. This is useful when determining the size between an adult and a child, which can be quite significant. When serving for a child, bear in mind the size of the child's hand in comparison to an adult, to

make sure they are getting adequate and appropriately sized portions in their day-to-day diet.

- Using the thumb rule when serving protein food, whether it is fish, chicken or meat, bean or pulse, it should be a palm size. A serving of vegetables should be no more than the size of a child's fist.

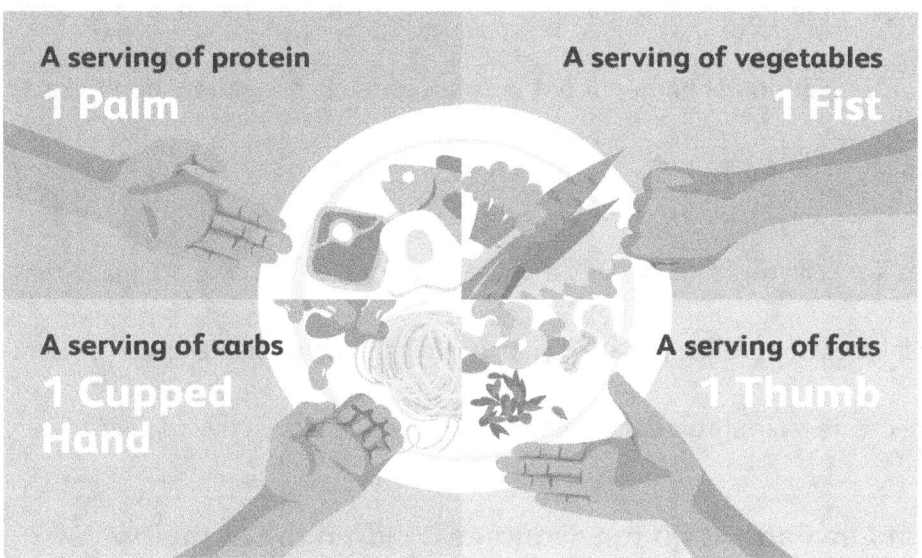

Introduce water at the earliest time so that children begin to love drinking water, not to only refresh their body but also to make them aware that water is the best drink/nourishment for their bodies. Once your child is of the age to eat solid food, around six months, you can introduce your child to fruits and vegetables. Offer a child a piece of steamed carrot in between meal, and other finger food that is mash-able between your child's gum. Allow your child to feed themselves, instead of spoon-feeding. This is a good way to get your child to start developing their fine motor skills. They should be able to use their whole hand to pick up food and put to their mouth.

If you give your body the best foods rich in vitamins and minerals, then will you not think it is going to benefit the mind as well? Yes, eating correctly also causes an effect on your mindset.

So, Your Child Is Fussy Eater

If you have a fussy eater, mealtimes can make you feel like you want to pull your hair out and it can cause a lot of tension within the home. It is very frustrating for parents to watch their child only fiddle with their food at dinner or not even touch it, claiming they "don't like it." Then what happens? Thirty minutes later, guess who is hungry? You guessed it. Your little fussy eater.

It is common for children to go through a phase of fussy eating. There are many reasons why this happens, so it is best to consider if there is an underlining reason. For example, a swallowing disorder, reflux... there can be a variety of reasons why a child is refusing to eat their dinner.

What Can Parents do to Encourage Children to Eat their Meals?

With children, the starting point is always their interest; recall times when they have eaten their meals. What was the meal? What were you doing? Were you placing a lot of emphasis on the need for your child to eat their food? What was the child doing? What were you eating? What happened before the meal? These kinds of questions may help you realize some of the things you or your child is already doing that will assist in them becoming a better eater.

Depending on the age of your child, you can involve them in the planning of the menu and preparation of the meal. If your child is two years and above, they can carry out this activity with adult support. Everyone pitching in to help prepare the meal is teaching your child some important family values and support your child to develop their skillsets. This allows for bonding family time and your child is learning to sort, measure, communicate, time, develop their knowledge and understanding, etc. In carrying out this activity, your child is less likely to refuse the meal they have helped to prepared.

MAKE MEALTIMES ENJOYABLE

Remove all distraction during mealtime and talk about things other than eating at mealtime. Dinner is a great time to talk to your child about how their day went. During breakfast, you could discuss what everyone has planned for the day. If your child is a preschooler, sit your child on a stable chair, with their feet supported (use a small step or telephone books if they can't reach the floor).

If your child is sitting in a highchair, remove the tray and allow them to sit closer to the table with the family and eat together. Your child is then exposed to a variety of foods they may not eat themselves and they can learn from others around the table. Offer food that your child enjoys on a plate and introduce new food on another plate. This is a good way to introduce new food every other day, but do not pressure your child to try this new food as they may find it challenging.

- Provide your child with choices around the mealtime. "Would you rather sit by me or by Daddy? You can eat with a fork or a spoon which would you prefer. Do you think you will need more potatoes or is that enough? Have as much as you think you will need to make it to supper. Would you like milk or water?" Try and maintain the child's diet throughout the whole time.
- Your child has to be comfortable with looking at and touching food before they will consider eating it.

- It is okay to play with food. Play is how children learn to tolerate different textures.

BE A GOOD ROLE MODEL. Let your child see you eating the food they have prepared, irrespective of whether You like it or not.

Reward your child for eating most of their meal or for trying any new food introduced.

"Good job. You should be proud of yourself." Too often, we only notice the negative aspects of our children's behavior and that is what we reinforce with our negative attention. Be patient with your child.

LIMIT SNACKING

For children to be hungry enough to eat a meal, they usually need to go two or three hours without food. However, it is difficult for children to go from noon to 6:00 p.m. without food.

A nutritious snack after school should be fine to get your child to dinner and ensure that they still have an appetite for dinnertime. Be creative in the ways that you dish up your child's food. Often, fussy eating children like their food to be set in a particular way on their plate, so mold mashed potatoes into a volcano, cut meat or sandwich into bite sized pieces and poke toothpicks in them, layout veggies in the shapes of letters or numbers, or use a drop or two of food coloring to make it more interesting. Children should eat around 5 times a day; 3 main meals and 2 snacks. Try to have mealtimes at the same time each day. Try to avoid long gaps between eating during the day or allowing a child to graze throughout the day. Be consistent in the boundaries set for mealtime.

Children need lots of nutrients to power their energy to keep them going. Fruits like oranges, strawberries, bananas and leafy greens like spinach, broccoli, carrots are packed with vitamins.

HEALTHY BODY, HEALTHY MIND:

Oral Hygiene: Children's healthy teeth and mouth are an important part of a child's well-being. Introducing your child to brushing their teeth should start when the first tooth erupts. Their primary teeth are important in forming facial structure, speech and for chewing and eating. Brush your child's teeth at least twice time per day, in the morning and before going to bed. Children should not wash their mouth after brushing teeth prior to going to bed as this allows the fluorine to continue working while the child is sleeping. If your child informs you that they are thirsty during bedtime, only give water to drink after brushing teeth before going to bed.

Why teach children to brush their teeth?

Healthy mouth and teeth are an important part of a child's well-being. Having toothbrush, paste and dental floss as part of the tools for cleaning teeth gets them in the habit of brushing their teeth. Maintaining oral hygiene can be a challenge for small children, if it's not introduced early into children's development. Teeth helps us to chew our food and assist us to talk. Having clean, healthy teeth has also become more important than ever before for taking our selfie pictures

It Is Never Too Late

If you have a pre-schooler and you have not yet introduced your child to brushing their primary teeth, it is not too late. Some children may not like to brush their teeth, or like the taste of the toothpaste. Start by allowing your child to hold the toothbrush and feel the texture of the brush. Always purchase the paste that is age appropriate for your child. A small portion of paste is required. Regular visits to the dentist at least twice per month are also good and it is important that you let your child see you brushing your teeth.

Sleeping Routine

Getting children into a sleep routine from an early age is beneficial to them. It promotes growth and is important for their physical and mental wellbeing. Children who get sufficient sleep are able to focus better, boost their learning ability; it also helps with improving their attention spans and improves their health, weight, and memory skills. When children do not get the right amount of sleep each night, these ever-important needs of a child will suffer.

A bedtime routine includes all of the things that you do with your baby or child just before you put them to bed, such as taking a bath, the last diaper change, putting on pyjamas, brushing their teeth and reading a bedtime story or singing a lullaby. Keeping to a routine of time, for example, going to bed, waking up, mealtime, bath time, helps children to feel secure and comfortable as they know what to expect.

The goal of a good bedtime routine is for your child to fall asleep on their own, without being rocked, watching TV, or having you lying down next to them. This way, if they do wake up later, they should be able to fall back asleep without needing any extra help. This ultimately helps both you and your child's sleeping pattern.

Sleep allows the body to rest and repair itself. During sleep, the body's muscles develop and the body releases hormones.

The amount of sleep required by each child will depend on the age of the child. On average, children need a minimum of eleven hours' sleep every night. A relaxing bedtime routine is important for children development and wellbeing.

Children who sleep well are more energetic, playful and focus. Lack of sleep can increase the risk of childhood illness.

Involve Your Child

We know that eating healthy is good for our physical health as it gives the energy that the body requires to carry out task. Involving your child in physical activities such as outdoor play, supports your child to develop strong muscles, hand and eye coordination skills, interaction skills, team building skills, just to name a few.

THE IMPORTANCE OF PLAY

The best toy your child has is you, a responsive parent that can interact and respond.

Play is the building block to the network of pathways that allows children to develop their capacity for complex thinking.

Children need to be given opportunity to engage in pretend play and develop their imagination skills, while, at the same time, learn to share and use equipment, explore roles, and model roles of adults. They must be encouraged to use language as a means of communicating and develop their independent skills by learning to dress and undress themselves

They can develop their problem-solving skills, along with the skills to form relationships and interact with their peers and socialise.

There are a vast variety of inexpensive materials within the home that children can use for play. Art material ranging from glue, paint and cardboard that can be used for drawing. Strengthen their fingers through the use of playdough.

Children learn by example and the best way to encourage children to be active is for parents and caregivers to be active.

Working with children and observing their habits have given way to my belief that parents play a vital part in ensuring that children are supported to adopt healthy habits. When children are encouraged to be active and eat healthy, they are more likely to stay healthy and grow up having less health problems. These are important roles to be played by parents as well as those working with children within the early years sector.

Outdoor Play

Outdoor environment provides a learning space where children can explore and be at one with nature. Playing outside games is a brilliant way to enhance children's learning abilities. They are an excellent type of exercise for your child. Children should participate in outdoor games to increase their energy and boost their stamina throughout the day. You will notice a remarkable improvement in your child's mood, fitness, and immunity level, when they participate in outdoor play. It increases their flexibility and strengthens their agility.

Your child's physical development is as essential as mental development. It exercises their bodies and minds. It allows your child to engage their senses while, at the same time, developing both physically and mentally.

Play supports a vital part of physical development in children and is directly linked to the brain's capacity. When children play with building blocks, they are learning to plan and build, make shapes and patterns, problem solving, learn about measures and compare. It is a means of communication and teamwork.

Benefit of Outdoor Play

- Outdoor play has shown to benefit children by giving them an outlet for excess energy
- Being physically active outdoors is a great way for children to have fun and exercise. It is also proven that exposure to sunlight improves moods and strengthens immune systems. It's not just beneficial to physical health, it is also great for mental health and well-being.
- Being in natural surroundings has a calming effect which leads to children feeling happier and healthier. It gives children the chance to escape from the stresses of everyday life
- It supports their communication, social interaction skills and problem-solving skills. Playing in peer groups give children the opportunity to learn valuable life lessons and skills that are sustainable, transferable and cannot be taught through classroom learning. It's an opportunity for open ending play, and a chance to explore new experiences, messy play and make new friends.
- It helps children to have a better sleep after spending time outdoor, enjoying the fresh air.
- Through play, children can learn to be sociable.
- Children learn to use their energy in different ways, and they learn to work as a team with each other when they can safely play outside.

- Growing up in Jamaica, I had the freedom of having a large outdoor space which provided opportunities to climb trees, rounders, skipping, and other activities. I learned turn taking and sharing. I developed independent skills while playing outside with my friends and those were the happiest times.

CHAPTER EIGHT: The PIZZAZZ Child

Understanding Your Child's Uniqueness

Nobody ever said parenting is an easy and smooth task. More frequently than is publicised, parents find it difficult, and frustrating at times to handle their pizzazz child. Understanding your child's uniqueness would definitely do wonders. Besides, if you won't make the effort to do so, who will?

Parenting has always been among the most significant and challenging jobs known to mankind. Understanding your child's need could help you discern and decipher what exactly it is your child is trying to say to you. Having a child with special needs can be challenging at the most. Often parents are unsure what to do in most areas of their child's development and are at a loss of how to approach this problem.

Our society places its expectations on perfection, so if something is not placed according to those standards, it's then said to be faulty and damaged. Even before a child is born, there are screenings that enable a parent to know if their child will be born with any disabilities.

For most parents and others, hearing the word disability is a dreaded word that builds up negative connotations of punishment, defect and disappointment. It becomes the elephant in the room that no one wants to talk about. It is an issue that many people find uncomfortable talking about.

In my years of working with children and in my own personal life, I have encountered some of the worst prejudice imaginable targeted at those without the power to defend themselves.

Being different does not mean you don't matter; a special child is a child with a bit more Pizzazz that you cannot devote your life to without loving them.

What springs to mind when you hear the word SEN (Special Educational Needs)?

On the 29th of May 1996, I went to my local hospital for an anomaly scan that checks the physical development of my baby. The 20-week screening scan looks in details at my unborn baby's bones, heart, brain, spinal cord, face, kidneys and abdomen. This was necessary because blots were seen on my previous scan. On this day, I heard the dreaded word "disability" mentioned in the same sentences with my pregnancy.

Fear gripped my heart as I lay there listening to my sonographer explaining her concerns, and what this would mean. At that point, I knew my life would never be the same.

My first thoughts were: did I do something wrong? Why is this happening to me? How am I going to explain this to my husband? (He was not there with me as he had to deal with a family emergency).

Nevertheless, I was determined to enjoy my pregnancy to the best of my ability. Every so often I would have a gentle reminder that there is a possibility that my child may have a form of disability. The uncertainty of what type of disability it would have caused me great anxiety.

Fast forward to the birth of my second child; a beautiful bouncy baby girl was born. Due to the concerns that was raised at my previous scan, my new-born baby underwent a variety of tests lasting for over a week, which resulted in doctors not being able to find anything wrong with her.

As she began to grow, delays were becoming noticeable in her development. She was later diagnosed with mild autism, speech delay and weak joints. Given that her disabilities were not physically noticeable, I experienced a lot of discrimination accessing services.

Autism is the king of all tricksters. I know this to be true because whenever I would go to specialist parent forums, the looks of disgust we received in response to our attendance spoke volumes. Unless we inform someone, and we always have to, no one has a clue that she is autistic.

If you want to know what an autistic child looks like, look at your own child or the children you are familiar with. Look at the children who live next door to you and take a glimpse at every child you walk past in the supermarket. These could very well be the faces of children with mild autism. There is no visible indication that a child is affected by this neurological disorder.

Like I mentioned earlier, there were always time when she was a toddler and I had to attend appointments. I would be in a room and after a while, I would come to the realisation that my daughter and I were the topic of discussion. The slight glares from other mothers and individuals who did not understand why we there and did not think autism was the reason for us being there.

One incident that stood out in my mind is a trip to the seaside. On this occasion, we were invited by the local support group to go on a family day trip. On the journey there, I felt the eyes of the other parents on me. After a while, a mother came over to ask why I was on the trip when my child did not have a disability. This was not the first nor the last time that I had to explain to people about my daughter's condition.

There have been so many occasions when I've had to defend myself against those who find it necessary to make rude comments or over stared. Sadly, amidst all of the open glares, the whispering and the challenges, my daughter is now a young adult and autism remains.

Autism (pronounced awe-tizem) is an illness that affects social and communication skills. Some autistic children have a hard time playing with others and making friends and some can't talk. Many autistic children display behaviours that may include, repetitively lining toys up, or spinning a toy, spinning around and not getting dizzy, not wanting to be touched or hugged, or wanted to be cuddled, not liking certain food items (arfid), which deals with the density of the food—if its wet or white. She had the ability to scream for hours. Of course, every autistic child is different. There are varying levels of this disorder and that's why it is called a 'spectrum.'

Autism challenges in my household range from fussy eating, endless crying to sleep time. When she was a toddler, mealtime was always a challenge in the home. Her dislike for certain food was remarkable, she didn't like food that were wet, she would push her plate away and refuse to eat. She did not like her food items touching on each other, so her food had to be made in a specific way. During her early years, she would have a specific name brand cereal that was eaten dry.

My way of getting over this challenge was to introduce one new item per week to her in a variety of ways. For example, adding vegetables into the main meal in a different format and putting fruits in her breakfast to ensure she was getting the right amount of nutrients.

Another challenge was her "Vision tunnel" as she was only able to see things from her point of view. She found it difficult to grasp another point of view. She would also get frustrated when she couldn't get her words out or I could not understand her point of view or need.

I learnt to give her the room to speak and agree with her for the moment.

I had to learn to work around her as she was unable to grasp another point of view. Agreeing with her and leaving her comes with loads of hugs and cuddles. I knew that she would always later return to apologise for her behaviour, when she has calmed down and had time to think about her actions.

Autistic children thrive on routine, so this must be in place in every area: one little change can mess up their entire system. For my daughter, she needs to know in advance what is going to happen: when she is not told, it throws her off balance, often causing chaos in the family home.

My daughter had the ability to go through a minimum of twenty dribblers within a twenty-four-hour period. This constant dribbling caused me great concern, and when investigated, it led to the awareness of her speech delay and inability to control her tongue.

When a child is unable to verbally communicate their wishes and needs, they will find other avenues of expressing themselves. She would take me to the item she wanted and place my hand on it, meaning I was to get it for her. After a while, she started to point until she was able to speak. When the words were un-clear, she would use her pictorial book.

Right now, no one expert has been able to confirm what causes autism, but one thing is certain: bad parenting IS NOT the cause of this impairment. Unfortunately, you still have some who are ready and willing to wave the idea around that a parent can inflict autism onto their child. There are a few people I knew who were quick to say that there was nothing wrong with my child and she only needed to be disciplined. Although such an accusation hurts deeply, I now understand that it doesn't matter who the person is or how well-educated they may think they are on the subject of autism; no one can truly comprehend what it's like to raise an autistic child unless they are raising one themselves.

Letting her live out the tantrums and frustration in a safe way was my way of coping with her.

Knowing the difference between the frustration of autism, non-verbal communication behaviour and the terrible two behaviour is completely different.

Dealing With Behaviour

Often, tantrums are only associated with the terrible twos but in having an autistic child, the tantrums can go beyond two years old.

Adults, stay calm it is never about you. I learned how to go into her safe space, depending on how she is reacting. Using a calm voice and gestures to reassure, like, "Ok, I hear you," being repetitive, calling her name to reassure her that it is well. I have to be mindful of my own body language and tone of voice while getting to her level and being patient with her.

Although I had given my children what I consider to be good parenting, their development was different, and they grew differently. I am happy to report that my second daughter, while still dealing with everything that comes with autism, is thriving and living her best life.

Often, children's misbehaviours and tantrums can drive parents crazy. This is particularly true if parents cannot seem to correct such misbehaviours. If you are facing this kind of problem, try taking the approach to solving it by treating the misbehaviour as a message. Your child may be trying to tell you something that he/she is struggling to convey verbally.

Managing Emotions

Socially organised behaviour is incorporated into our parenting. It involves our child's ability to read social cues, but this does not mean looking at ways to punish a child's behaviour. It is a guidance strategy to achieve corporation. With children that are challenging, this is one of the most effect tools to use to get their cooperation, which is what we want from our children. We don't just want their obedience; we want their participation and patience in the goals we are trying to achieve for their development.

Just because a child has no verbal language does not mean they are not communicating.

My daughter has the ability to process her emotion into communication and then transfer that into relationships. Most of her emotions are locked up, so trying to unlock that and get her to communicate with me how she is feeling can be difficult at times.

As a parent, I found out that for me to get her to talk, I first had to be prepared to listen to her having a dialog using que social behaviour.

Building on our relationship through trust

When she is challenging, become more flexible, use negotiation system as a means of communicating, use calm guidance strategies and use positive tones that build connection. She needs more time than my other children to adjust to change which takes time and can cause her to experience frustration.

I see her behaviour as a way of reaching her on a one-to-one level to get her to improve her opportunity for growth and change.

Children display their feelings and emotional anger by crying, hitting, having tantrum episode, just to name a few, some of which may not be age appropriate.

Children go through stages of feeling anxious as they develop and grow. They may display worrying or difficult behaviour, some of which can be short-lived, while some remain with the child for a longer period.

Age-Appropriate Expectations: Behaviours

Children normally behave according to their age. If we as parents have too high an expectation from them and looking at their developmental age, what will happen is that the child will exhibit frustration and so will the parent. Both adult and child have different expectations. If not done properly, it sets the stage for situations to occur that will cause the child not to succeed. Behaviours that should be expected from five-year-olds as against a three-year-old child are different.

It is impossible to count the number of times you will see a child misbehaving when they are out with an adult, only to hear the adult respond to the child by telling them to stop behaving like a two-year-old. The problem with this sentence is simple: if the child is a two-year-old, then he or she is behaving age appropriately.

While, on the other hand, if the child is a five-year-old and he/she has not been taught to behave appropriately then that child is still behaving appropriately because they do not have the skillset to manage specific feelings and emotions.

Is this behaviour outside of the norm? A child who is not interacting with peers, or a child who is displaying tantrums by throwing themselves of food items on the floor and kicking at adults are all signs of typical child behaviour that is seen by an adult as not normal or not expected. What should be done about this and is it a concern?

Children are all different: you may have a child that is an introvert, or another that is an extravert.

Psychologist Carl Jung describes these two types of personalities based on their ability to regain energy. Introverts requires minimal stimulation and alone time to recharge. They are quiet, reserved, and thoughtful in personality. Extraverts refuel by being with others and they are often referred to as the life of the party.

Where one type of behaviour is normal for one five-year-old, it may not be normal for another. This will depend largely on the skills that the child has developed or learnt. Knowing what is normal is important, and most often it is the adult's behaviour that is problem.

Worrying about difficult behaviour can be short-lived. Sibling rivalry is part of the norm and adapting to change in the family environment can trigger a change in behaviour.

Talking to your child about the behaviour they're displaying and allowing the child to explain what is happening will help you to know how to help. Often, the child has an idea that could help solve the problem they are experiencing.

Younger children who are not able to put their feelings in words will display their feelings by hitting, biting and pulling down things, because they are not developmentally able to share what is happening for them at that moment.

A typical two-year-old whose language is not fully developed will display this type of behaviour. At most, this is due to frustration the child is experiencing and the lack of verbal language. So, when the child sees another child with a toy that they want, a two-year-old will not go up to the other child to ask for the toy; instead, they will snatch, bite or scratch the other child to get that toy.

Toddlers and siblings at the age of two are not yet able to share; they are bossy and strong-willed, and their favourite words are "mine" and "no."

This is normal for a two-year-old. If a five-year-old was to demonstrate the same behaviour, then unless the five-year-old was taught to ask or wait his turn for the toy. This is the expected behaviour of a child that has not been taught.

Ways To Support Children's Behaviours

The way we talk to babies tends to differ according to culture and social advantages. As your baby grows and develops, using words with your child from your vocabulary is encouraged. Although the child may not at first understand the word, hey can grasp the concept of the meaning of words. Older children might not want to talk at first, so it is best to take it easy and allow the child to understand, by giving example of what you mean. For example, you can say, "When you said you hated Mummy, you looked really mad. What was making you so cross?" With a little encouragement, the child will open up and communicate their feelings.

Just as we do, our children have feelings and experience difficult situations. By actively listening and participating with our children as they talk about it, it demonstrates to them that we do care, we want to help, and we have similar experiences of our own that they can draw from. Remember, it's about responding, not reacting.

Don't discourage your child from feeling upset, angry or frustrated. Our initial instinct may be to say or do something to steer our child away from it, but this can be a detrimental tactic. Again, listen to your child, ask questions to find out why they are feeling that way, and then offer potential solutions to alleviate the bad feeling. Children need to work out their frustration in a safe way.

When your child's feeling sad, angry or depressed, communicate openly, honestly and patiently with them. Listen to them without judging or criticizing. They may not fully understand why they feel the way they do, so the opportunity to communicate with you about it may be what's needed to help them sort through a difficult situation. Sometimes, as adults, it may be just about us listening.

The best way you can support your child to deal with their behaviour is to teach them the expected age-appropriate behaviour.

Chapter Nine: Technology and a Digital World

We live in a world that is dominated by technology; in most homes, some form of technology device can be found.

When we speak of technology, we are referring to a product, device, skill and knowledge that we use to support our needs.

Whether it is through our television, laptop, console game, or mobile phone, we all have access to a piece of technology and use it in our everyday life.

There has been an alarming increase in the use of this great instrument since the last two years, even so much more during the COVID-19 pandemic. Masses of people are turning to technology to support their livelihood, corporate businesses, retails and personal needs. Families and friends have been spending more and more time on their devices and rely heavily on it.

Today's children are already growing up in homes with an ever-increasing array of technology devices. Parenting has never been easy, but the widespread usage of smartphone and other devices and the increase in social media and its influence has brought additional challenges to parenting.

One of the most debated topics amongst parents are about the correct amount of time that children should be allowed to spend on their devices.

Most adults of the twenty-first century will argue that today's children are spending too much time on their devices.

How Much Is Too Much?

The issue is not the devices that the children have in their homes, it is the content children have a gateway to and parental management that brings about the heat to the debate. Parents often are not aware of the content or understand the dangers their children can be exposed to as their children are accessing various sites. How this device is used by children in the homes can be the issue at hand.

Furthermore, a lot of the twenty-first century parents are not as technology suave as their children and this puts them at a disadvantage as some parents or carers are unable to keep up with their children. Because of parents' lack of knowledge of how to access their children's devices or the password, this puts parents at a disadvantage.

From birth, children have some form of technology device to keep them calm or deal with emotions. For example, most baby cots can be seen with a mobile musical device attached, or inside the cot there is a musical lullaby.

These devices have become a substitute for parents in the sense that the musical instrumental devices have now replaced a mothers' embrace and cuddles for bonding, comfort and sleeping time. YouTube videos often replace parents' quality time spent with their child as it is often used as a form of 'babysitting.'

It is no wonder that the millennium babies are suave in using these devices. It has become their world, and the attachment to digital instruments is a must for our growing 'yummy mummy fad.'

Another issue that many parents have with technology devices is that, when compared with reading a book to a child, they don't require the use of critical thinking, a great deal of imagination, or communication skills. Therefore, children are not acquiring social interaction skills.

This leaves parents urgently desiring to know whether digital technology of the day is harming their child's mental health, cognitive behaviour, physical health and development or whether technology devices are beneficial in most forms for their children.

What Impact Does Screen Time Has on Our Children Development?

When we speak of screentime and the negative aspect, we straightaway think in relation to its impact on children. As children have been spending more time on their devices there, has been an increasing awareness of harm to children's health.

Many parents fear that letting their children have more than an hour or so per day 'screen time' will turn them into a 'socially obese couch potatoes.' Parents are fearful that smart devices will hurt their children's chances and ability to do well in school to attain the skillsets to be creative and pursue their hobbies and interest. For example, kids are easily distracted by their iPad to the point that they don't want to do their homework or if they do their homework, they are rushing it so they can get back to their iPad.

Another concern for most parents is around their child being the target of bullying or harassment, sexual exploitation and accessing violent content.

Yes, the more time your child spends on a 'screen device' increases the risk of it becoming a harmful tool to the child's health and mental wellbeing. However, it is the parental control that will be the deciding factor to the protection and guidance of the child.

There is an expectation from parents to monitor the amount of time their child spends in front of screens and on other devices. However, there are a large percentage of parents that struggle with the usage of digital devices or they also are distracted by the same, and they too have become victims of distracted parenting. It is my opinion that both parents and their children would benefit from spending less time on their device and use the time communicating and bonding. This can be a rich experience when parents are able to listen to their children with no distraction. Lately, technology has robbed most parents of this beautiful experience of knowing and understanding their children.

The overuse of mobile phone devices can be harmful to your child's health, as the more your child uses their mobile, the less physical activities they do. Furthermore, when children choose to play on their devices instead of going outside for outdoor play, this is often accompanied with unhealthy snacking, which can lead to significant increase in weight and other associated health problems. The recommendation is that children should not have screens— television, phones, laptop—and any other technology devices in their bedrooms, especially at nights.

It is a cause of sleep deprivation. It is recommended that all screens should be turned off at least an hour before bedtime and read with children before settling to sleep.

It is not the use of technology that is bad for children, it is how that technology is used and the amount of time being spent on technology that has a negative impact on their lives. Research by Julia Calderance on August 20, 2018, claims that as children spend more time tethered to gadgets watching YouTubes videos and listening to music through headphones, there is a potential chance that these devices are harming children's hearing and eyesight. Children can experience eye discomfort, fatigue, blurred vision, headache, and other symptoms of eye strain from too much screen time.

There are several ways a child can play with their smartphones, and other games devices that still foster the development of their creativity. Games are here to stay, so rather than fighting them, why not use them to your advantage?

Imagine a World Without Technology

We live in a world where technology has become part of our everyday life and without these devices, we would struggle to do even the simplest of tasks. Our dependency on technology has skyrocketed and has boiled over onto our children. Instead of buying workbooks from the shops or even reading books, a lot of parents are turning to online apps.

Parents play an important role in ensuring that the app or device chosen for their child is beneficial. Quality time should take precedence over quantity of time.

Children grow up fast, so it's up to parents to make each moment count. The more time your child spends on a technology device, is the less amount of time your child spends with you or caregivers. Children may not be able to identify the risk of using technology for long periods of time, which is where parental explanation comes in.

It is the parents that are best placed to monitor the amount of time children spend on their device and to recognise the harm children may face when long period of time is spent on screen. Ensure that the programmes your child is accessing are child friendly and appropriate for their age and development. Set boundaries around what your child watches. Most importantly, explain to your child why you are putting these rules in place because they like clarity as it gives them understanding and reasons to think then ask questions. Provide children with the positive and negative effects that technology will have in their lives.

Technology is here to stay, and it can be an incredibly helpful tool for families to embrace, when used correctly. It can be the vehicle of educational learning for overwhelmed parents, to help structure children's learning in a personalised and meaningful way plus provide support for children. It would be unrealistic to think that children will stop using technology, but with appropriate guidance and monitoring from adults, children can be taught to enjoy this great tool. Children and technology are our future, so when harnessed correctly, parents can guide their tech-savvy children into a brighter future.

Let's get some rules in place to keep our children safe and give us peace of mind to the future of living in a digital world.

First-hand, I have seen the magic of connection during this pandemic as technology has thrown us a much-needed lifeline. In the last two years, our relationship with technology has seen a paradigm shift which changed our approach to the way we think adapting to the new ways of advanced technologies.

No longer is technology seen as a value-added addition, but as a vital part of our infrastructure and a necessity to aid life within the tech culture.

Strategies to Allowing Children to Enjoy Technology Safely

Discuss with your child the importance of safety whilst using device. You have heard me mention previously the importance of establishing boundaries and putting them in action—the key is for everyone, including parents, to sign up! Boundaries can include no devices in bedroom, or other parts of the home after a particular time. No devices at the table during mealtimes so family can enjoy quality family time. Be consistent!

Devices should be switched off and put away at least half an hour before bedtime, so everyone can enjoy time together before sleep time.

Be a role model for your child to see, so keep your screen time in check as well. Give your child your full attention when they are speaking to you and listen to what they are saying. Do not become distracted by your mobile phone.

Take an interest in the games and other activities your child engages in on their device; after all, what could be more fun than creating an actual computer game with your child? It is fun, it is bonding, and clearly shows your interest in what your child is doing. Children respond to this act of love.

CHAPTER TEN: Shaping Future Parents

The children of today will be the future parents of tomorrow. They will grow up to be the leaders, doctors, and politicians of tomorrow.

Our children *are* the next generation, and we are passing on a legacy to them—whether for good or for bad. The burden of care is upon today's adult, so we must give careful consideration, therefore, to the quality of that legacy, how we raise our children and the values we instil in them.

What parents need more than anything else is to recapture a strong sense of value and beliefs to teach their offspring what will benefit them and create a succeeding generation. However, we live at a time when there is much confusion about how parents should go about this task.

One of Most Adults' Comments About Children of Today is:

"Today's children are different!"

I disagree because children are the same but what has changed is a society with its fast-paced living, lowered expectations, standards, lack of discipline, acceptance of disrespect and a generation thriving on technology that impact the ethos of the family and community.

Surely one of the most important duties of parents is to raise with children morals.

We have a duty to benefit and serve our society as best we can, and that includes how we prepare the next generation. I strongly believe that the best place for children to learn to lead is an environment in which they are actively participating in all aspects of learning. While I agree that there are times when parenting seems like an insignificant task and parents are fighting a losing battle. Especially when parents have to deal with sleepless nights, nappy changing or arguing with teenager about curfew, or tidying their room. However, parenting is one of the most rewarding and important job. It can be challenging while at the same time pleasurable.

Think about the importance of raising children who are obedient, who grow to have mature character and healthy self-regulation, develop healthy relationships with others. These are the reasons why parenting is so important. Of course, there is no such thing as the perfect parent. However, by God's grace we do our best to support them to develop the correct attitude, by being aware of your child's emotions and support them to go through each phase correctly.

Adults' starting point is to teach children godly morals, how to respect others and to educate them about taking responsibility for their actions. Teach them that everything in life comes with cause and effect, so that they are adequately prepared to become leaders of the future.

When we give children boundaries, rules, limitations, rewards, and consequences, they have an idea of what is expected of them. They will rise to the challenges and exceed our expectations as parents! Of course, love and boundaries go together. These two factors are the key predictors of the kind of parenting that produces children most likely to adhere to their parents' values and most likely to have the capacity to establish and maintain positive relationship with others.

In the long run, children need most of all to know there is nothing they can do or say that moves them away from the love of their parents.

The strategies in this book will also change your view of how-to parent children and will shape the future.

Imagine if we never taught our children the basic skillsets, what would their world be like? They need to be taught how to strengthen their mindset by doing simple activities. For example, jigsaw puzzles or open-ended games that will extend their problem-solving skills and broaden their cognitive development. Always encourage them through learning and praise.

Adapting to Change

Children are very resilient and are more adaptable to changes than adults. This means it is easier to get a child to change their behaviour than an adult. However, if left too late, then children can also be hesitant to changes.

The earlier we can set the behaviour we want the child to exhibit from an early age, the better and easier. It will be more difficult, if we wait for the child to get older, to teach them to change and adapt.

What if from an early age we teach children age-appropriate behaviour? The quickest way to get a child to transition from one thing to another is to explain what is happening. This allows the child to experience less stress and lessen the number of tantrums.

Would you not rather have a child who is compliant than a child who is emotional due to being side-tracked or unsettled. Why make things harder for yourself when you can give them the right start by putting in place all the skillsets they will need to grow into responsible adults.

Start by easing them into transition by preparing them for upcoming events and explaining to them what is happening and why. Getting their support can prove helpful. I know what you are thinking—that they are too young to understand what is happening—but this can't be more far from the truth.

Even though they may be young, they like routine and often a little bit of compromise goes a long way in getting children to accept and cooperate.

Think about the times when you as an adult was unsure of what was happening for you. How did that make you feel? What about when you went to an event and didn't know anyone there? You were surrounded by strangers and not told what was going to happen next. What about when you started a new job but was not shown your office or how to use the equipment? Where would that leave you, or more to the point, how would that make you feel?

Unless you do something about it, those feelings are only going to build and grow worse over time. The longer you take to get your child into learning these skillsets, the more you're likely to regret it.

Not to mention the very fact that you're responsible for growing our future generation. After all, who would you rather grow your child and teach your child all the importance skillset for their future? It is really no contest.

Parenting in Today's World

As parents, we always want the best for our children, and we want to give them all the things we didn't have growing up ourselves. This all boils down to the fact that we feel an overwhelming desire to make a difference and to change things.

Of course, none of these matters, unless you are prepared to do the things that matters most and give your child the greatest start that will allow them to reach their full potential.

How Do You Do That?

So, you start with a clear understanding by teaching them to dream big and believe in themselves. As a parent, you have a critical role in helping your child mature and have a view of the world that we are created for relationships.

Ask yourself the question of if you want your child to be concerned about the needs of others and have a kind and caring souls, to begin to model the ideals of empathy, kindness, altruism, and selflessness. All these are the key ingredients that tap into our divine aspect of human nature. It also allows your child to see these values in you.

You can demonstrate this principle by conscientiously pointing out to your child the difference their actions make and how it affects others around them. Reinforce, point out their positive responses, etc., and reward them.

My friend always states that you should teach a child the way they should grow and when they are older, they will not depart from that teaching. Therefore, in your evaluation of the things that matters, you want to keep in mind things that get you excited when you were growing up and captures your interest. The memories that you cherish and values you hold.

The reality is that if you don't put these things in place, your child will struggle to cope in an ever-revolving world.

It's all about the attitude that we portray and how you chose to grow you child. In the end, you have the choice of nurturing and growing a child that is not on an emotional roller-coaster but a stable, caring child with the essential skillsets that are best learnt by seeing you living them out.

They will see someone who is hard working, exceed others expectation and willing to go the extra mile for others. Someone who is confident, and capable to adapt and make changes, plus admit when they make mistakes and stay open to new ideas and ways of doing things.

Leaving a Legacy

A wise man Said:

"Don't be afraid to start over again; this time, you're not starting from scratch, you're starting from experience!"

In the future, survival will depend largely on the ability to adapt in a fast-changing environment and that is why you need to teach children to do things!

Oftentimes, we think of giving children chores as a list of things they need to do at a specific time. They are tasks set to improve, grow and develop children's independence. Your child may be doing some of these already, like helping to take out the trash, washing dishes or unpacking the dishwasher, tidying their rooms, putting away their toys, doing the laundry, etc.

These are the steppingstones to building a foundation of taking care of themselves, their future, their environment, and the things that they will need to do to pave the way for a healthy adulthood.

In fact, doing these things, according to research, is laying the foundation and the prediction of adult success and happiness. Show me a parent who doesn't want their child to grow up being happy and successful!

It doesn't mean that if you have not been doing these things with your child, you should go all out to doing everything. You can start small with simple steps to ease your child into doing chores in the home, and as your child grows and develops, start adding extra into their routine.

Remember you are helping your child to succeed. All these strategies provided will ensure a better tomorrow for all.

CONCLUSION

Parenting is one of the most challenging occupations throughout the world, yet, in its own way, is unique to each parent and each child.

The parent and child relationship is the catalyst of importance that teaches the child the fundamentals of establishing 'the foundation' of communication to be built upon. Not all parents can do this under the same roof; however, with support or professional intervention, relationships can and do improve.

Nicole Bennett-Blake stresses that children learn within the boundaries of a healthy parent and child relationship. She mentions the importance of holistic growth and child development to love, accept love, understand they are valued and understood. Also, the fact that adults should validate the child's emotions and help them to understand and respect boundaries, rules and consequences through day-to-day interaction, communication, and guidance.

Problem solving is dotted through this book. The key to The Parent and The Happy Child is to master the tips offered and consistently being opened to discuss with your child any issues raised or recognized. This, with no doubt, will continue to nurture your relationship deeper and leave a legacy to be passed on.

HAPPY READING and LEARNING!

Bibliography

Bruce, T. (2005) Learning through Play babies, toddlers and the foundation years. Hodder Arnold

Whalley, M. (2nd ed) (2007) Involving Parents in their Children's Learning: Learning Power Kids. Paul Chapman Publishing

Leach, P. (1997, 3RD ed.) Your Baby and Child: The Essential Guide for Every Parent. Penguin Books; Harmondsworth.

Lindon, J. 2007 Understanding Child Development London Hodder Arnold

Internet (Google search)

Toilet Training: when and how to do it Raising Children Network retrieve

Mercedes. S. 24/06/2020 Encouraging Your Kids to Play Independently Retrieve from https://www.(parentingforconnection.com)

Surprising Reasons Why We Need to Discipline Children (verywellfamily.com)

4 Ways to Set and Keep Your Personal Boundaries | Psychology Today 04/01/2022

Child Health Academy (hello@marketing.healthprofessionalacademy.co.uk)

Don't Let Your Children Fall Short of Their Potential-Next Generation Institute (nextgeninstitute.com)

YouTube Videos

This is a selection of videos that I personally found useful.

Foundation stage - videos and leaflets. This video has some useful footage to highlight what should be happening with and for 3-5-year-olds.

Preschool Learning Binder - learning the basics to support toddlers learning in preparation for reception.

How to teach children to take turns - can be used with children who are not yet verbal.

Building attention skills in Children: The Bucket - teaching children how to zoom into using language to develop their communication development.

Judy. A. How to teach your 1-2-year-old toddler to build their fluence and patterns for reading.

How to speak or interact with children; Children are Humans.

Toilet training: when and how to do it | Raising Children Network

Parenting In Today's World - Shame proof Parenting

Essential Character Qualities to Help Your Child Reach Their Potential – Next Generation Institute (nextgeninstitute.com)

Acknowledgments

First and foremost, praise and thanks to the Lord, the Almighty for His direction in leading me to complete this book successfully.

I would like to say a big thanks to DMJ Publishing and all those who contributed to the creation and success of the physical book. My agent, Gerry Roberts from Black Cards Publishing who gave me the golden opportunity to realise my dream of becoming an author. My book coach, Leesa Landry, for her support and the marketing team headed up by Daisy. My editor, Maxine Ivey, for her continuous strive for clarity of a higher standard— Maxine has helped me with researching topics and coming to a better understanding.

Thank you to my pastor, Daniel Barnett, who helps me to continue to strive and grow in my leadership qualities and other areas. To the parents and staff of Nicki Day Nursery Ltd for providing an environment that brought out my expertise.

To my good friend and my sounding board, Pastor Devon Phillips, for always being there when I needed to reflect and put things into prospective. I would like to thank him for his empathy, friendship, and sense of humor.

Thanks to Reverend Fitzroy Williams for giving me the opportunity to share my experience with others on his podcast (DCM.T.V).

To my best friend, my mentor, my go to person, Samantha Toussaint, who helped to pull this book out of me. All attempts of this book could not have been satisfactorily completed without her support and guidance.

To my family who put up with me and helped me throughout the arduous process of writing this book: first to my husband, Craig Blake, who has been a tower of support, and my three beautiful daughters, they supported me with their continuous prayers. Their love, patience, and understanding in the areas of technical software that I struggle with.

I thank my parents for the quality of parenting, discipline and core values they instilled in me.

I would like to express my special thanks and gratitude to my niece, Charlene Savoury, for her continued support and encouragement.

I am extending my heartfelt thanks to everyone for their interests shown in the completion and success of this book.

Nicole Bennett-Blake

RESOURCES THE AUTHOR RECOMMENDS

Name: **Nicki Day Nursery**

Address: 190 Southampton Way

Postcode/City: SE5 7EU, London

Camberwell County:

Greater London England

Phone: 020 7708 2738

Mobile: 07538 676840

Website: www.nickinursery.com

A place where children are happy and settled and show a sense of belonging through their developing self-assurance. They are delighted to see their friends when they arrive, greeting one another with smiles, hugs and lots of conversation. Their individual needs are met. Children's behaviour is very good as they learn how to share and play cooperatively with peers.

They benefit from a wealth of praise and encouragement and compliments offered by practitioners which have a positive impact on their self-esteem and sense of belonging. Children thrive on responsibility such as being the day's special helper which contributes to them being positive and productive.

We are the National charity for homeless people. We know that homelessness is not inevitable. We know that together we can end it.

We provide vital help so that people can rebuild their lives and are supported out of homelessness for good. Together with homeless people and Crisis supporters, we campaign for the changes needed to end homelessness for good.

www.crisis.org.uk

Tel: 0300 636 1967

Crisis UK (trading as "Crisis") is a registered charity and company limited by guarantee. Registered charity Nos: E&W1082947, SC040094. Company No: 4024938

We are an Accountancy practice in the United Kingdom established since July 1986. We understand the needs of our customers and serve them in the following areas: Audit, Self-assessments, Bookkeeping payroll and accounting services

Independent Examination Self Assessments Tax Returns Budgeting and Forecasting Tax and VAT Returns Bookkeeping Financial Statements and Accounts

Payroll Administration Company and Charity Registration CIS Reclaim Business Advice Pensions-Auto Enrolment

A registered Charity that addresses the needs of small voluntary and community Sector organisations including faith groups.

Training / Work Placements Tel: 020 7708 5999 E: admin@laplondon.co.uk

Mob: 0780938188 Website: www.laplondon.co.uk SOJOURNER TRUTH CENTRE, 161, SUMNER ROAD, LONDON SE15 6JL

TESTIMONIALS

Mentor

I am so grateful I had the opportunity to grow and develop with Nicole.

Nicole has been a mentor and a mother to me for over forty years.

She has shown her ability and her strength at a very early age. Extremely helpful and caring to everyone. She has a brave attitude to reach out to people in a positive light.

Nicole has worked in all areas of childhood development and has inspired us all to reach our full potential.

With her wealth of experiences, she has mastered the art of being one of the most dramatic persons by helping adults and children to build and transform their lives to the highest standard.

As a mentor and mother, she has personally helped me to grow and reach my full potential as a pilot and community ambassador.

I really appreciate her and am extremely happy that she has reached out to the world with her book to help and motive people and share her life skills.

Reading this book will help us all to grow in love and develop all the techniques in life that we need to build ourselves and our relationships with our children.

Lady Lesa Crossman-Thomas

During my son's nursery years, I had the pleasure of meeting Ms. Nicole. My son has been in her daycare for quite some time, and he enjoys it so much. He gets excited to go every morning! When I drop him off, he can't wait to go play and learn with the other children! He loves the owners and the staff, especially Nicole– the owner. Nicole loves children, she will make sure your children are looked after very well. The staff are very professional and extremely friendly to all children. It is a very loving nursery. I have never had a problem with any of the staff or owners not telling me what my child has been up to during the day... they have always told me what my son has done and accomplished. Ways, I can better support him at home. For example, he was not verbally communicating, and she gave me strategies to use so he could start to use speech.

(David) Nursery years, he has been able to learn how to express himself better and learn how to communicate his feeling with his family in a more meaningful way.

He is able to reflect on his actions and share with us all his concerns on a daily basis. It has truly started the development of his communication skills.

If I find I am concerned about his development, Ms. Nicole would always find time to speak with me and encourage me.

I am very pleased I came across Ms. Nicole.

Thank you, Nicki, for all your support and love towards David's journey.

Luciene Santos' mum.

About the Author

Nicole Bennett-Blake is obsessed with levelling the playing field. In 2021, Nicole embarked on her journey to become an author to share her life's passion for teaching children and building connection in relationship and learning.

Nicole has two degrees, her first in Social Work *BA Hon (2002)* and Early Years Professional Status (2011), both obtained at the University of North London.

Nicole Bennett-Blake began documenting her experiences, learnings, and resolutions and is now an accomplished author and CEO of Creative Ideas Solution since 2021. She is also the owner of an established Children's Nursery for over fifteen years and currently managing Nicki Day Nursery Ltd.

She is a strong advocate for children and is best known for supporting parents with high-energy children. She involves herself in the well-being of children.

Nicole is known for her work, knowledge, experience, and love for children. She has been a noteworthy leader in her profession and in the position of being a manager. Her professional interests focus on her latest books: *Evangelism Made Simple* and *Stop saying Yes*. Her current projects include her soon to be released book: *The Good Parent and The Happy Child—A Guide for Parents Caregivers and Early Years Consultants*.

Nicole is actively involved in her local church as part of the leadership team and is the director of the evangelism department.

She is actively involved with a local charity organisation called CRISIS UK which supports homelessness.

Nicole enjoys spending time with her family, going on holidays, and taking long walks as a way of relaxation and reflection time.

Nicole Bennett-Blake is married to Craig Blake and the couple lives in South-East London with their three daughters: Avon 31, Letisha 25 and Paris 19.

www.ingramcontent.com/pod-product-compliance
Lightning Source LLC
Chambersburg PA
CBHW081710100526
44590CB00022B/3724